To/ Timothy, from Daddy.

28th. May 1987.

(Hope you get a chance
to have a go.)

GW00499029

Still-water Fly Fishing
For Young People

Still-water Fly Fishing
For Young People

Sidney du Broff

Photographs and illustrations
by Nedra du Broff

Kaye & Ward Ltd. Kingswood

For Nedra,

Who fished with me on our
honeymoon,

And for all the young people who will
hold a fly rod.

Published 1982 by Kaye & Ward Ltd.
The Windmill Press,
Kingsworth, Tadworth, Surrey

ISBN 0 7182 2280 6

Typeset by John Smith, London
Printed in Great Britain by
Whitstable Litho Ltd.
Whitstable, Kent.

Illustrations

1

I'm Sidney Du Broff – call me Sid. Let's go fly fishing for trout on still water. We've got the lakes, and we've got the trout – waters created by man that sparkle like diamonds in the sun, but more precious, more valuable. Now these waters are almost everywhere in the land, available, ready, waiting for us to come and drop our flies onto them.

You may have seen people fly fishing, casting with the grace and precision that is so much a part of the fishing itself – and felt, more than anything, that you would like to cast a fly that way, too.

Maybe you have seen the fish strike, seen the rod bend, watched the fish break water and hurl itself skyward in an effort to throw the hook. You could almost feel the fish tugging at the line with all of its strength – and a rainbow trout has plenty – and wished desperately that you were holding onto that rod.

And why shouldn't you wish it? It's a beautiful way to fish – exciting – rewarding. The excitement of it will never leave you – whether you are taking your first fish, or your thousandth. Your heart will beat rapidly, and your hands will shake, and in the end, maybe, you will bring in that fish.

How old do you have to be to start fly fishing? Some people start at age eight – and some even before. If you can hold a fly rod, you are old enough. If you are a girl – and you think you would like to come along, too – you are more than welcome. Don't let anybody tell you this is a sport for boys or men only; it belongs to whoever wants to hold a fly rod in his or her hand, and cast that fly, filled with hope, out onto the water.

But there are some things you are going to want to know – need to know – before that is actually going to happen.

As younger people, varying in both age and experience, your problems are of a particular nature. This book has been created to answer your needs, and to make you a more knowledgeable and confident fly fisherman. You will be better prepared to go out and catch some of those trout that have been stocked for that very purpose – whether you have yet to grasp a fly rod in your hand, or have already experienced the thrill of dipping your landing net under many a fish.

Life will be easier if your father is a fly fisherman, or if you have relatives or friends who are. Hopefully, at least, your parents will be sympathetic. This counts for a lot – in providing finance, transport, and co-operation generally. Fly fishing is not cheap, though in some areas it may be cheaper than others, with, often, concessions being made to help younger people. In the Thames Water region, those under sixteen years of age don't have to buy a Water Board licence. This is usually the case in other regions as well. In addition, young people are often given substantial reductions on day and season tickets.

FOR PARENTS

Parents are inclined, generally, to be helpful, in so far as they are able. They are deeply aware of the many benefits that fly fishing must give their children, which includes a closeness to Nature that no other activity can provide. It creates a deep and absorbing interest, wholesome, constructive, teaching co-ordination, and a grace that is the hallmark of fly casting.

Those young people, standing on a bank-side, casting their fly, I am eager to point out to parents, are very unlikely to want to waste their time in activities that are socially destructive. The pursuit of fish is basic; it follows what must be a primitive desire and need, inherent in many, though not necessarily in all – men and boys, perhaps, to a greater extent than in girls and women. Men have been the hunters – hunting for food – on the land and on the water. Those who fish are answering that ancient call. To do it with a fly rod is to have refined the method – and to do it in what is undoubtedly the most effective manner of all.

8

2

In fly fishing, perhaps more than in many things, there is a lot of controversy. It covers almost every phase, including the tackle, and its usage. There are many choices when it comes to tackle. For a newcomer this creates confusion and anxiety. It's not difficult to make a mistake, and that can cost money. In the end you don't have what you want or need. The variety of tackle that exists is meant to answer the needs for particular circumstances and conditions. But without knowing in advance what those conditions and circumstances are to be, choosing the proper equipment is next to impossible.

I have been through this problem myself as a young person, and I remember very well, and painfully, the frustration that was endured. Everybody seemed to know the answer – except me – and nobody appeared to want to tell me. "What kind of fly line should I get?" I recall asking the man in the fishing-tackle shop. "It depends what you want to do with it," was his reply. Other than catching fish on it, I didn't have the vaguest idea regarding its specific application. I didn't know what options I had, and finding out was a long, and often painful, process.

Writing this is a deep-felt need, perhaps even an obligation – to those who are as I was; I do it with great pleasure. If I can make your path easier – the one that ends at the water's edge – then I am pleased. Eventually, with the passage of time and the benefit of experience – I will be able to learn from you. Your experiences will contribute to the sum total of our fly-fishing knowledge. I will never know it all. Each time I fish I learn something new – and so will you.

I'll tell you how I do it, what works for me, why, and when. You will catch fish. Eventually you'll do what suits you best, what provides the greatest satisfaction and reward. And reward there will be – the kinship, the oneness with your surroundings – the marvelous feeling of being a part of them which those fishing hours will provide. They are precious hours, cherished hours, because for most of us, they are so few. We must make the best of them, the most of them.

3

The development of our still waters is one of the great English achievements. Everybody has gained, and nobody has lost. At least from a trout fishing point of view we live in a marvelous era. We who fish those still waters have a very large debt to those who created them, who fought to make them into trout-fishing entities, and who maintain them for our pleasure. Don't ever take them for granted. Nature was far from generous when it came to making lakes in this country. But man has stepped in and done what Nature failed to do. It is up to us to cherish and protect those waters. They are man's gift to man, and to the environment. Probably there is one of these created waters near you. They include reservoirs, often very large ones, like Grafham Water in Cambridgeshire, over 1600 acres, and Rutland Water in Leicestershire, the biggest in Western Europe – 3000 acres. And gravel pits, from which all the gravel had been removed, and were turned into lakes, which were stocked with trout. In addition, people have literally dug lakes out of the ground – Avington and Damerham in Hampshire are such waters – and stocked them with trout. That they are not natural is in no way to detract from them; nor is the fact that the trout are stocked and do not breed naturally. It is an example of man managing and controlling his environment.

Still-water trout fishing is a relatively new development in this country, though man-made still-water lakes – reservoirs stocked with trout – have been in existence for many years. Probably two things have contributed substantially to the development of still-water trout fishing in England and Wales – the rainbow trout, initially imported from the United States in 1882, and increased economic prosperity. The rivers could not accommodate those who wanted to fish for trout on them, particularly in an industrial society that had given over so much of its effort to polluting its waters – not to mention the agricultural one that is no less guilty of pollution.

The trout they stocked – usually more rainbows than browns – could be grown in ponds to almost any size before actually being released into the lakes. By comparison, they made those river brown trout look like tiddlers, which in fact they were – running four to the pound, and often less – but seldom more.

The serious fishermen got down to it, learned how to take trout from a lake – studied their habits, what they ate and when. They developed new techniques, and flies, fly lines and rods.

4

If you are an impatient person – that's just fine. This is not a game for the patient – but for the restless spirits – eager to be successful in the hunt. Patience will not be rewarded; on the contrary, it invites defeat. In this pursuit something is almost always moving: your fly onto the water, then retrieved through the water. If it is not effective, it will soon be replaced by another fly. Then, if you are dissatisfied with your location, you will move yourself to another part of the water where you think you might do better.

Though you may go fishing with others, you catch fish, or don't catch fish, by yourself. It's up to you. You are on your own. In the end, it has to be a solitary effort. Fly fishermen generally prefer solitude, though they may normally be very sociable people in all other ways. There is great pleasure in this solitude for many, in the sound of stillness. Fly fishermen, taken as a whole, are a pretty good lot – helpful, considerate, generous. What more can we ask from our fellow man – and what more can we be in return? As a person new to the sport, you are in good company. Ask for assistance, and you will get it.

Now let's get down to practical things. If you don't already own a fly rod or have access to one, you're going to have to buy or make one. It should be a minimum of nine feet, going up to nine-and-a-half, but not over that. A longer one can be ungainly. Don't buy a shorter rod because you have not as yet attained your full height. Today's fly rods are sufficiently light to permit proper usage for even the very young.

There is a lot of admiration expressed for cane rods, and rightly so, beautifully-made creations that are examples of supreme craftsmanship. But keep it to admiration, and buy a man-made fibre rod. Usually these are smoother, easier to handle, cast better, and wear longer. They are also lighter and cheaper. A good glass rod will serve well, but if the finance can be arranged, a carbon fibre will do even better. It is also possible to make your own rod. Instructions follow later in the book. Boron is the newest space-age material to be used for fly rods. It is stiffer than carbon, but costs are considerably higher.

You want a rod with a reel seat below the handle, with locking rings that move on threads, and lock the reel securely into place. Pass over the kind with rings that merely hold the reel to the cork handle of the rod; those rings have a tendency to slip – usually when there is a fish fighting at the other end. The handle, made of cork, should be at least seven inches long. If the handle is protected by a piece of plastic, tear it off the moment the rod becomes yours, since keeping it on will make gripping the rod more difficult, and will trap moisture underneath it, eventually injuring the handle.

The wider the diameter of the rod rings, the better. There should be one of them for every foot of rod, not counting the tip. The maker of the rods designates the line for which it is best suited, and it is stated in writing, usually, on the rod, just above the handle. I want my rod to be able to handle a number eight or nine line – that's a pretty heavy one – we'll go into lines presently.

FOR PARENTS

For most young people, money is a factor, particularly since it is usually the parents who have to put it out. There is a certain understandable reluctance to invest heavily in equipment which may be used only for a short time, and then put aside if the interest wanes; and there is really no way of guaranteeing that it won't. Nevertheless, I believe in buying the best quality possible under the circumstances. Good equipment will produce better results, insure to a much greater extent the success which is being sought. A cheap rod is hardly more than a toy and will not function adequately. This, in turn, will increase the chances of failure, which is to insure that interest will dwindle, and soon disappear. At that point parents will congratulate themselves on not having invested a lot of money when the interest was not sustained. However, that interest probably would have persisted were there to have been results that did not end in failure and defeat.

Later in the book we will tell you how to make your own rod.

That rod will need to be a pretty stiff one, able to propel line into the wind and across it, as well as with it. The idea is to catch fish, and many, if not most of them, will be caught in wind conditions that are difficult. Therefore, you need a rod that is up to the job.

Now comes the line. This can be the hard part. But we're not going to let it be hard. I'll tell you what I do, what works for me and what I recommend. In due course you may find you want to do something else. You just go right ahead. By that time you will have become sufficiently knowledgeable to know what you want to achieve on the waters that have now become familiar to you. For that Number 8/9 rod get a Number eight or nine slow sink, weight forward line. That's right, *slow sink*. This is bound to cause controversy since it is a floating line that is usually recommended. You can't get a sinking line to float, they will tell you, but you can get a floating line to sink, by using a long leader, and attaching a lead shot to it. There is truth in this argument, which does have a certain amount of validity. There are those who never use anything but a floating line – and you'd be surprised at how many of them hardly ever catch anything, except perhaps when the fish are on or near the surface, which isn't often.

In all truth, most fishermen carry two rods with them – two complete outfits – one that is meant for fishing on top, the other for fishing well below the surface. There are those who may even carry three complete outfits with them, which includes a sink-tip line – I am one of them. Eventually you will probably have more than one outfit, too. It is possible that you already do now. But if you don't, and for the time being, at least, one is all that you can cope with, then it should be the slow sinker.

As I recall last season, I could have thrown away my floating line altogether and not have caught very many fewer fish than I did. A slow sinking line gives you far better control over where you want your line to be in the water than a floater with a lead shot attached, which I regard as an emergency measure. Not long ago at Avington in Hampshire, fishing the First Lake, I took a fish early on. A man standing nearby asked what I was using. It was a kind of nymph of my own creation. He had something reasonably similar and put it on. But he didn't catch anything on it. A couple of casts later I took a second fish, and not long after that, a third.

By this time the poor man was in something of a state. "Have you got another one of those things?" he asked eagerly. "I'll buy it from you."

"I've got another one," I said, "and I'll be glad to give it to you." (Good sportsmen don't sell their flies to other fishermen on the bankside, but are only too pleased to present them as gifts, if they have them to spare, particularly if they have made them themselves.)

He took the fly with profoundest thanks and dashed off to attach it to his leader. He cast it out and waited for the fish to strike it. But no fish did – despite the fact that I took my fourth and limit fish on that same fly. He was using a floating line. I told him that the fish were deep; though he used a longish leader, and my fly was tied with copper wire to make it sink more

14

adequately, he still may not have been getting down deep enough. Retrieving the fly probably caused it to rise, and ride higher than it should have in order to be effective, though much of the water at Avington is not particularly deep.

5

Many fly fishermen feel compelled to use a floating line. They feel that by doing otherwise they compromise themselves and appear to be less good sportsmen. This is a concept that has its origin on the trout streams, and is often a carry-over by those who want to reproduce a trout stream experience on a still-water lake.

You have come to catch fish on a man-made lake, and you will want to use whatever method, or methods, will help you to that end – whether it is with a floating line or a sinking one. Stay clear of a controversy that has no basis in logic.

During certain times of the year, and for periods during the day, trout will be feeding on, or just below, the surface. A floating line will indeed be a handy piece of equipment, and when you are able, get one. But it should be your second line. There may very well be times when you want to put your fly on the top of the water and keep it there or just below. Many people fish this way and find it productive. You may, too. We will discuss methods later. But remember, we are fishing lakes, not rivers or streams, and what we say here is pertinent only to still waters. If you have access to a river, enjoy it. What you learn here may or may not be helpful.

The number designation on the line is the weight – the bigger the number, the heavier the line. You want a heavy line because it cuts through the wind. And wind is one of the things which you will encounter on an English still water more often than not, even on days when elsewhere it is not particularly apparent. The lakes are usually at the lowest point in the area, which gives wind – and cold – the opportunity to build up there.

That weight forward line suggested here is one, as the name implies, that has its weight at the front. It will enable you to make good long casts; the line will streak out into the water. The slow sink line allows you to fish close to the surface, merely by beginning your retrieve as soon as the fly hits the water. You can also fish mid-water, or scrape the bottom if you wish, by allowing more time for the line to sink.

There are also fast sink lines, most useful in very deep water where you want to reach the depths quickly, mainly on the large reservoirs.

The floating line may also be a weight forward, but can be a double taper. This means that both ends are tapered, and when one end goes, you can reverse the line on the reel, and have, in effect, a new line. It has an economic advantage, though my own preference, again, is for the weight forward line, since I like the way it casts.

Without trying to complicate matters, but in order to try and present a fair amount of the picture, if not the whole one, there is also a sink tip line. The front part of it sinks – usually the first ten feet – though one company, in order to achieve greater depths, makes a line that has its first fifteen feet go under. Because of the two densities – the difference in weight between the part of the line that sinks, and the part that floats – it is a more difficult line to cast. It can, however, be extremely useful at times, particularly on small waters, where you want your line to go down, but not too far down; where, when retrieving slowly, you want your fly to remain fairly level, and not sink to the bottom. There are those who contend that it has no application on still water, but is a line more suitable for salmon and sea trout on rivers. I strongly disagree, but as far as you are concerned, for now, and for the immediate future, it is not a line you will want to seriously consider for your own use. However, the time may very well come when it might have an application as far as you are concerned, and you would want to know of its existence.

Another line is the shooting head, meant for achieving distance casts, and made from thirty feet of a double-tapered line. About a hundred feet of monofilament is affixed to the back end, and about thirty feet of it to the front. A shooting head can sink or float, depending upon what you want to do with it. It takes a fairly competent caster to use it properly. I personally am not all that keen on it; it seems to cancel out the basic essence of fly fishing, which is an expression of grace. Besides, I – and you – can achieve almost as much distance with a normal weight forward line.

Fly lines are expensive. It is possible to get mill ends in the weight and type you want fairly cheap. I have used them, and have found, by and large, that they are not worse than their more expensive and branded counterparts. But, with an unbranded sinking line, for example, you can't always be sure in advance of the speed at which it sinks. These lines are available from some of the large mail order discount tackle houses. Check the fly fishing magazines for their advertisements that give specifications and prices.

6

The reel need not be expensive. A single action of good quality will do the job. But don't get junk in order to save money, because it's going to fall apart, and that will ruin your fishing day.

Now you've got your rod, line and reel. You need some monofilament of twenty-pound breaking strength, about twenty-five yards of it. This is meant for backing. Attach it to your reel with a blood knot, as illustrated.

Wind it on to your reel. Attach the back end of the monofilament to the back end of your line, using a needle knot, as illustrated. Wind the line onto the reel. You will want the drum filled almost to capacity, which will make for a quicker rate of retrieve.

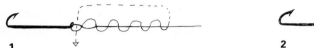

1   2

The Blood Knot

This is an easy knot to tie and very effective. I always use it for attaching the fly to the leader. Thread the leader through the eye of the fly. Hold it with your left hand (presuming you are right-handed), and wind it over the monofilament in four turns, as in Figure 1. If it is new monofilament, not yet having been in the water, it is going to be stiff and somewhat more difficult to work with, so hold it securely.

Put the tail through the loop at the eye. Hold it with the thumb and index finger of the left hand, and pull. It will all come together, as in Figure 2. Be sure to leave enough tail. Pull hard to test it. The harder you pull, the more secure the knot becomes. Cut off the tail. It's done.

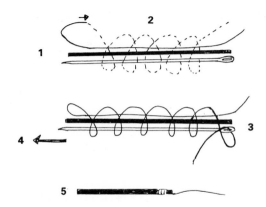

The Needle Knot

The needle knot, while not difficult, is going to take some practice, and you might not get it right the first time around. Don't worry. For one thing, you are using heavy monofilament, which is going to be stiff, and will seem to have a mind all its own. Soak it in water for a while to get out some of that stiffness.

A lot of people push the needle through the fly line, though I can see no need to do so. The method illustrated has always worked for me and has never come undone.

Lay your fly line on top of the needle. Lay your monofilament over the line, leaving yourself a goodly tail. Figure 1.

Wind the monofilament over line and needle, making five turns, as indicated by the dotted lines in Figure 2.

Push the tail through the eye of the needle. Figure 3.

Now pull the needle. Figure 4. This is the crucial part. It can all come undone here. If it hasn't it should be like Figure 5. Trim off the tail.

Each turn of the monofilament should lay evenly along the fly line, with no bulges that will make it difficult to slide through the guides when you are bringing in a fish.

18

To the front of your line, attach five feet of that twenty-pound-test monofilament, using the needle knot. Tie a simple loop at the end of that monofilament.

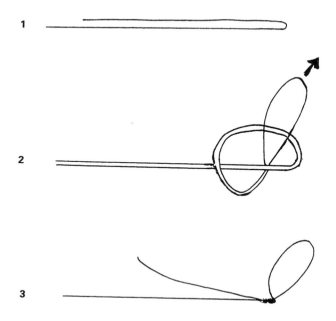

1

2

3

The Loop

Here is a knot that won't give you any trouble. Lay three inches of monofilament back over itself. **Figure 1.**

Create a loop an inch back from the end by laying the monofilament over itself, **Figure 2,** and bringing the first loop through it.

Pull, as in **Figure 3,** and trim off the tail.

Easy, wasn't it.

Assemble your tackle. Attach a leader to the twenty-pound mono. How much of it and how thick is something we will discuss in detail later. For now it isn't too critical – let's say four feet of seven-pound breaking strength; no need for anything tapered.

Do you know how to use the equipment? Ideally, attending a class with a competent fly-casting instructor is the best way to learn. In the beginning I admit to having had a certain amount of scepticism about going to a

Sid helping a young friend on the Common.

class to learn to fly cast, but the years have shown me its many advantages. Check your nearest fishing tackle shop and the fly-fishing magazines to see where and when classes are being given.

If your father, relative or friend can give you instructions – that's fine – providing he is not only a competent caster, but a good instructor. It's one thing to know how to do it yourself, and another to be able to teach somebody else how.

If you can't get anybody to teach you, turn to the place in the book where instructions are given, and let's go down into the garden – if you have one and if it's big enough – or to the Common, if it isn't. But first, tie a piece of red wool, or other brightly coloured wool, to the end of that leader. The point of this is to help you to see exactly where your leader is; if you were on the water, this would indicate where your fly has landed.

If you go out on the Common, be prepared for the remarks that passers-by will find impossible to resist making: Have you caught anything? How many have you caught? Don't you know there aren't any fish on the Common? Smile bravely and carry on. There is no need to take offense. And no offense is meant. Just possibly you might also get some valuable help; a knowledgeable fly fisherman, seeing you in the process of teaching yourself to cast, might stop and offer assistance. Do accept it. You will know soon enough how good he is by the progress you are able to make.

20

7

Now we need some flies. The best method of obtaining these is to make them yourself. Again, father, other relatives or friends might be able to teach you. If this is not possible, then there may be a class going in your area. Some schools run evening classes in fly tying. Attend one if you can. There is a very considerable amount to be learned. It is recognized that tying flies is a legitimate subject to be taught in a publicly-supported institution. However, if such possibilities do not exist for you, then, when you are ready, turn to the section on learning to tie your own flies, and we'll show you how. Learning on your own, from a book, is much more difficult than getting even a few lessons from someone who can show you the fundamentals.

I feel that it is important for you to tie your own flies – ultimately – though in the beginning it is okay to start off by buying them. For one thing, tying your own flies will bring you much closer to your fishing, and will, consequently, make you a better fisherman. You will tie them as you want them, weighted if required. You will deviate from the standard patterns if you wish, limited only by your own imagination to create new patterns. They will be based on your own observations and experiences on the water.

The flies you make are also cheaper than the ones you buy, though, in all honesty, I am not convinced that tying your own flies will in the long run save you money. There is the initial cost of the equipment. There is also the constant need to acquire fur, feathers, wool and tinsel – all the bits and pieces that can be tied into a fly.

More than likely, the flies you make will be stronger than those you buy. Some of the commercial flies have been made in great haste, with quantity, rather than quality, the goal. This can be rather disturbing, when, within a relatively short time, the fly starts coming apart. You are going to make some rather heavy demands upon that fly, when you stop to think about it, under difficult and extreme conditions. Firstly, it begins travelling through the air at a hundred miles an hour. Then it is flung onto the water – perhaps hundreds of times – and then pulled through it. It may encounter water weed, branches or other snags in the course of being pulled along. It may also encounter a fish, a trout with formidable teeth who can wreak amazing destruction on your fly. When it happens this way, you don't feel quite as bad as when the thing starts to unravel all on its own.

The hook, too, is subject to all sorts of stresses and strains, and unless it is of a good quality, it will break at a critical moment – when the fish has that fly in its mouth. If – and when – you lose a fish, always check the hook, to see that it hasn't broken or been straightened out by the fish. Otherwise the next one will get away, too. You want a forged hook, which means that the running surfaces of it have been flattened on both sides. Sometimes professional fly tiers try to save money by using low-quality hooks, which means you will have to pay twice – for the fly and for the lost fish.

These are amongst the reasons you will wish to tie your own flies. You will probably reach the point where you will feel confident only with your own flies at the end of your leader, having little faith in those tied by anyone else. There will of course be exceptions to this; the odd fly that you exchange with someone you encounter on a bankside, a fly you discover in a tackle shop in some remote place that works its magic on the local water. Or, conversely, fails to work on the local water, but performs amazingly on some other lake.

You may even become so proficient at tying flies that you are able to supply tackle shops with your creations, or perhaps have your own clients, whose faith in your work is so great that they become dependent upon your efforts. Good flies are always in demand. Now is the time to start collecting the feathers. You will find these during the course of fishing, on the land and on the water – swan feathers, duck, goose, rook. Put them in see-through bags or envelopes, marking what they are. You might also find the odd bird that has encountered a fox or other predator, with only the feathers remaining. Snip them off with your scissors and save them.

If you are a shooting man, or know someone who is, your life will probably be filled with feathers and fur. Save it all. If possible, keep the entire cape or fur. We'll tell you how to do that, too. You might be able to develop an exchange programme in feathers and furs, bartering them for other things that you might need with friends or the local tackle shop.

8

Speaking of tackle shops, is there one near you? Hopefully it will have a goodly selection of fly-fishing equipment. Hopefully, too, it will be staffed by personnel who are themselves knowledgeable fly fishermen, and who are prepared to give you some of their time. In their own interests they would want to cultivate you; your requirements as a beginning fly fisherman are fairly extensive, and will become even more so with the passage of time. In many shops they will be quick to recognize this, and make every effort on your behalf, particularly when it becomes clear that you are serious about your intentions. You will be taken seriously, which is as it should be, and your youth will in no way be a deterrent. In shops with personnel that have a genuine involvement, you may very well be advised not to make a purchase, since your experience might not as yet warrant your so doing. But on the other hand, if they can't be bothered with you – don't bother with them. You are spending your money. Go where it brings you the best value – where they are prepared to do more than take your money in exchange for goods.

9

Start off by looking at flies – in the shops, at pictures, and, if you can, in the fly boxes of other fishermen. You may have heard anglers discussing flies, naming them by name, and telling of the results they have enjoyed, or failed to enjoy, on them. Perhaps to you, as a newcomer, the names were just names and had no significance. Eventually you will learn the names, which is a part of the language of the fly fisherman. It is important because it communicates what may be happening at that very moment, information that is highly pertinent to you.

Flies are charged with emotion – those bits and pieces of inanimate fur and feather – tied together. Moved through the water – they come alive. They embody the hopes and aspirations of their users. It is here where you win or lose; here where that fish will strike; here, at the end of your line, where it all happens. Consequently there are almost as many points of view as there are fly fishermen. I know one man, a very able still-water trout fisherman, who uses only three patterns – a Whisky Fly, a Baby Doll, and a Viva, and catches a lot of fish. Others may confine themselves to half a dozen or a dozen patterns, and take all their fish on those. On the other hand there are fishermen who bring hundreds of flies with them to the water, representing many patterns. They may only use a few of the patterns for the most part, but they are prepared for any eventuality. It's nice to have a dazzling array of flies, particularly when we have tied them ourselves.

What happens to the man who goes through his few patterns and fails to take fish? I suppose he keeps trying, persisting with those flies in which he has confidence – then he moves to another part of the lake, and tries over again. And what happens if still nothing happens? Then he goes home without fish.

I personally like to have a variety of flies at my disposal. The flies that brought success last week, more than likely, will be spurned this week. I remember, early on, I had great success with an Orange Muddler Minnow, taking a limit on it in a relatively short time – and it was the only limit on the water that day. Well, obviously, an Orange Muddler Minnow was the answer. But the next time, about a week later, they wouldn't touch it. So, that wasn't the answer. Every day has its own answer – and the problem is – to find it.

The reason is that the water in which you fish is a living thing. It changes, with the wind, with the temperature, with the seasons. It evolves, playing host to the multitudes of creatures that live in it, both insect and minnow life. It is upon this life that the trout feeds.

I change flies often, sometimes after three or four casts. If I am casting over fish – and on small waters that are decently stocked, the chances are pretty good that I am – there is no point in persisting with a fly that has been seen and constantly rejected. When I put on a new fly, I put on new hope. To change your fly is to be reborn.

But what flies do you want? I will suggest a variety, which, hopefully, will cover many of your needs. Each body of water fishes differently, even those close by to each other. The changing seasons see the appearance of new insect life, which the fish then consume. Not that trout won't take something new, or different, and – on occasion – only something that *is* new or different. On some water, only the conventional will do, and to lash out with something wildly different is a waste of effort. Whereas, on other waters, the sight of something not hitherto seen by man or beast is the best way of insuring a limit.

Here is a list of twenty-five flies. A lot of fish have been caught on them, some for two hundred years or more, others only within the past five or ten. But they work. Not always, and not all the time. But then, nothing does.

The Flies

PETER ROSS

INVICTA

BLACK ZULU

DUNKELD

BUTCHER

BLACK AND PEACOCK
    SPIDER

SILVER MARCH BROWN

CORIXA

SEDGE PUPA (available in
    several colours – brown,
    orange, green, cream)

PHEASANT TAIL
NYMPH

MIDGE PUPA (black)

MAY FLY NYMPH

DAMOSEL NYMPH

BLACK CHENILLE

VIVA

WHISKY FLY

OMBUDSMAN

JACK FROST

BABY DOLL

APPETIZER

JERSEY HERD

BLACK MUDDLER

WHITE MUDDLER

ORANGE MUDDLER

POLYSTICKLE

I have included three muddlers, often very effective.

Become familiar with all of these flies. Be able to pick them out by name. It might be argued that some of these flies could be left out of your first twenty-five, and others substituted, but the conditions in which you fish are going to be varied, so you will be covered for most conditions to be found in this country for the whole of the season. In this game there is very little that can be said for certain, and beware of those who make all-embracing statements. The fish have a way of upsetting set ideas and notions; this is a game filled with contradictions, changes, and the need to make alterations. The key to greater success is not to be rigid. There are always alternatives, and, during the course of this book, we will consider them.

10

Let us have a quick look at what flies are meant to be, and to do, and what goes on in the waters you fish. Flies are without a doubt the most effective way of taking fish – much more so than spinning or even using worms – and much more fun. A worm is a worm, but those twenty-five flies mentioned above are twenty-five different things, all of them meant to tempt a trout, offering him a great variety of things. If he doesn't happen to feel like worms, then the worm fisherman has had it, and if he doesn't feel like chasing a spoon, the spin fisherman has also had it. Trout are highly selective, and never completely predictable. Were it to be otherwise, there wouldn't be any still-water trout fishing in this country, since those who fished for them would all soon take their limits, and the fishery operators would all be bankrupt.

The size of the fly is an important factor – sometimes. When the weather is cold, trout eat less, going down to almost nothing at all. This is Nature's way of protecting the species, since in the cold months there is less about to eat. The metabolism of the trout slows down considerably. There is little food about, so, therefore, little is required. Even in the stew ponds, where the trout are reared, they do not take what would be given. But as the weather warms up, and aquatic life becomes available in ever-increasing amounts, the metabolism of the trout speeds up, and he begins to require more and more food, which is of course available.

In the spring and autumn it is often the smaller flies that do best. When the water is warmer the bigger flies will also be taken. For rainbow and brown trout, the peak feeding temperature is 60°F water temperature. Their active range is between 50°F and 65°F water temperature.

On many of the reservoirs, three-inch flies are common, and take fish.

These are waters that have had coarse fish enter them – roach or perch – that may well become a trout's dinner – and may easily go six inches. On many of the small, private waters, however, there is often a limit imposed on the size of the fly that can be used – an inch at Avington, for example, an inch and a quarter at Latimer – not a serious restriction.

The trout is a cold-water fish. If the water gets too warm we're all in trouble – the fish, the fishermen and the fishery manager. Trout begin to die when water temperature gets to about 80° F. Such things rarely happen in this country, though the drought conditions of several years back resulted in some losses, and came within a few degrees of catastrophe. The oxygen levels in the water were extremely low. If the water gets too warm, trout feed minimally, as the metabolism again slows down, Nature's way of protecting the fish during such conditions by reducing its need to move about. Energy is conserved. Less oxygen is required.

Trout eat the insects they find in the water, probably to a greater extent than the fry, except during September and October. On some waters the insect life becomes less abundant; there are fewer hatches now, so the trout concentrate more seriously on the fry. However, I have fished waters where the trout spent the whole of the fishing year making forays on the fry – to such an extent that the shoals of fry literally jumped from the water in a frantic effort to escape. The first time I saw this happen I was some distance away; I couldn't identify the silver strands that were making their way through space in their efforts to escape. On this particular water, fry were obviously an important part of the trout's diet. As in so much else that is pertinent to trout fishing, it depends upon the water, what else might be available, and the inclination of the trout itself, a factor very difficult to fathom.

Terrestrials are the insects that don't actually live in the water, but may well come to fall into it, and wind up as a snack – beetles, bees, wasps, caterpillars – any of the insects that live in trees overhanging the bank, and might fall in. If you haven't as yet had the opportunity to observe the fish feeding under trees that hang over the bank, you certainly will eventually, and it will present you with an opportunity to take your fair share of them.

28

The water-borne insects constitute a large part of what fish eat – in all of their stages of development – as larva, pupa, and winged adult. In their pupal stage they are known collectively as nymphs, as represented by the Sedge, Midge, May Fly, Pheasant Tail, and Damosel Fly. Most of the nymphs can't go anywhere on their own, except up or down, since they lack the equipment. They do a lot of wiggling, but they go where the water takes them, as determined by the wind and current. This is very important to us as trout fishermen, since the movement of a fly in a manner perceived by the trout as unnatural, will discourage him from taking it.

The Invicta represents a hatching sedge, which has now developed wings and will soon fly off – to mate, to lay her eggs upon the water, and then to die, which starts the cycle over again. An aquatic beetle is represented, for example, by the Black and Peacock Spider. There are those who might tell you that trout take a Muddler Minnow because they think it is a pellet – upon which they had been fed during the time they were confined to ponds prior to release. Nothing could be further from the truth. For pellets to be really effective, they have to be splashed out onto the water in handful lots. Trout take a Muddler for something that at that moment in time appeals to them.

Not that flies do, or need to, represent something specific in order to be successful. That they provoke is sufficient. Trout take flies because they think it is something to eat; because they are curious; because, as predators, they wish to express aggression. The fact that a yellow and red streamer fly may be incongruous both in itself and in its surroundings may be sufficient reason for the trout to hit it.

11

Does the fish see your leader? The clearer the water, the more apt they are to do so. But when intent upon feeding, this may not be a problem. There are those who fish with the finest leader possible – two, three, four pounds – an advantage when the water is clear and the fish skittish. But the disadvantage is obvious: a good fish will break it. On some waters there is a minimum breaking strength which may be used – usually six pounds. It is felt that a thinner leader is to invite being broken – by a fish which may never strike again.

At Avington, on one occasion, I was using ten-pound breaking strength leader – getting follows, but no takes. Avington is a big-fish water and I feel more secure with a heavier leader than with a lighter one. However, concerned that the thicker leader might be visible, I went down to six-pound breaking strength, and in a little while took two rainbows in rapid succession.

On the other hand, on one occasion at Latimer, I got a good fish on, using what for me was the normal six and a half pound breaking strength leader. I probably would have brought the fish in successfully had it not been for the weeds. I could see the fish several feet below the boat; it went four pounds easily, possibly a bit more. I really wanted that fish. Not much separated us – just a six and a half pound leader. But that was a lot. The leader was wound around the weed. It snapped. That was the end of my four-pound fish.

After that I went onto ten-pound leader when conditions were weedy and never lost another fish that way. Admittedly, at Latimer, it didn't seem to make that much difference about thickness of the leader. When a good-size fish went streaking across the water, even when there were weeds about, I felt confident that my leader would hold.

30

The leader, like the line, will cast better if it is heavier. If wind is a factor the heavier leader performs better, and is less likely to knot up. The length, too, has to be considered; a shorter one is easier to handle in the wind. When the wind was well up, I have used as little as eighteen inches of twelve-pound breaking strength leader. This is tied to the twenty-pound B/S five-foot leader that is permanently attached to the fly line.

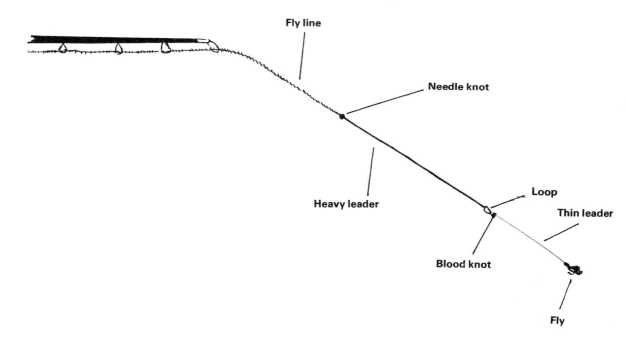

The Set-up

Your fly line is attached permanently to 20-lb. breaking strength of monofilament with a needle knot. (Attach a new piece of 20-lb. monofilament at the beginning of each new season.)

Make a permanent loop at the end of the monofilament, to which you attach your thin leader, with a blood knot. Then attach your fly to it, with a blood knot. If you have tied your knots correctly, and tested them, you can feel completely secure that nothing is going to come undone.

You will need more than one thickness of leader. Start with a spool of six-pound B/S and one of ten-pound B/S and make whatever adjustments your own experience will in time indicate.

Under conditions that are not especially difficult, I add another four feet to the existing five. I find this quite adequate, though there are those who use leaders of sixteen feet or more, but usually on a floating line, to make the fly sink to a greater depth. The longer leader will cause problems in handling, and greatly increase the chance of wind-knots, which substantially weaken the leader. If that leader should be broken by a fish, it will happen at the knot. So, if you can get the knot out – a pin might do the trick – do. If not, cut the leader past the knot, if it won't make it too short. If it does, change your leader. Leader material – monofilament – is amongst the cheapest items you are forced to buy, particularly if you get it in fifty or hundred yard spools, so it isn't worth trying to save money by retaining a piece with a knot in it. Keep your monofilament out of the sun and away from heat. These are what destroy it.

12

You need a scissors. It is an absolutely essential item. A nail clipper will do as well. Teeth are not meant for biting through leaders. Get the kind of scissors that has one arm pointed, the other rounded. These are available in the sewing department of most stores. Or get one that has both arms rounded. But don't use one that has both of its arms ending in a point – to avoid getting stuck. Affix a leather thong to it, or a piece of string, and wear it, or the clipper, around your neck as if it were a necklace. It can also be attached to the ring of a fishing waistcoat. Wearing it this way, I have easy access to it, and do not have to fumble in my pocket when I want it – and I want it a lot – since, as I mentioned, I change flies frequently. This

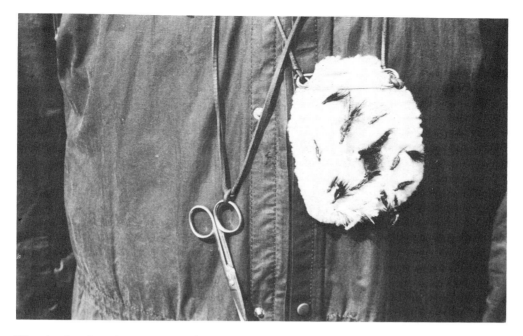

Tie a leather boot lace to your scissors and wear it around your neck for easy access.
Attach a kilt pin to a piece of sheepskin – an off-cut will do – of any reasonable size. Tie
the other boot lace to the kilt pin, and wear it around your neck, along with the scissors.
You now have a fly patch, to which you can attach your flies after use.

means that I also change leaders with a fair amount of frequency – as they
grow constantly shorter.

Around my neck, I also hang a sheepskin patch, particularly if it is cold
or raining and I don't have access to the patch on my waistcoat. It too is
worn like a necklace, held with a leather thong – a boot lace does very
nicely – a pair of them for the two items. I use the patch for hanging my
flies, upon being removed from the leader. It is handy for drying them (if it
isn't raining), to see quickly what flies have been used, and to have easy
access to them should they be required again.

For holding my flies, I like something small enough to keep in my
pockets – an aluminium clip box with an extra leaf, or a sheepskin wallet.
Some fishermen carry large wooden boxes, lined with polyfoam. This is

rather nice – your flies aren't crushed together and you can see them readily – but carrying it in your pocket is out of the question and access may be somewhat more difficult, except perhaps if you are fishing from a boat and have the array spread out before you. You would have to keep such a box in your fishing bag.

Speaking of bags, you need one. I like a fairly big one, though I wage a constant battle to keep my equipment small and minimal. It should have pockets – the more the better, a shoulder strap, and, if possible, a handle. Ultimately it's going to need to be washed. Those trimmed with leather suffer from being in a washing machine. What specifically I carry in my bag, I'll go into shortly.

Regarding boots, some waters allow wading, others not, so that thigh waders will see you through either situation. You can turn your waders down for ordinary bank and boat fishing, pull them up for wading, or if it should rain.

As a matter of course I wear overtrousers. They keep me dry, warmer, and my trousers clean – this will help to keep the car seat clean. If you prefer not to wear overtrousers all the time, the kind that fold sufficiently small should be carried with you in your fishing bag.

You will also need a landing net. It should be sufficiently big to allow a good-size fish to drop into it. A man I know, who always carried a rather small landing net got a big fish on one day – larger than any he had had before. It soon became apparent that his small net couldn't cope with it. Since he was in a boat, and nobody was close by, there wasn't anybody to whom he could turn for help. He was a very able fisherman – and played the fish out, longer than he probably would have had to do had he a proper landing net. And remember, there is always the danger of the fish throwing the hook – right up until the moment he is scooped out of the water; many a fish is lost at the net. He got the fish up close to the boat, its head out of the water, pointing skyward, reached for the gills and clamped his fingers through them firmly. He brought in the fish. It weighed ten and a half pounds. Besides being a pretty cool character, he was a very lucky man. In the process of reaching down to clutch the fish's gills, it may well have made a final lurch, and snapped the leader. A fine fish would have been lost.

Landing a fish by this method is not recommended. Make sure you have an adequate landing net. My choice is one that folds flat when not in use, with a clip that can be slipped over the ring on your fishing bag or your belt. You want a sufficiently long handle to enable you to reach out a fair distance, particularly in summer when the weeds can sometimes be pretty heavy close to the shore. Many who wade stand their nets up in the water by pushing the handle into the lake bottom, keeping their nets upright, ready for immediate action.

Sunglasses are of great value in protecting your eyes. Polaroids help you to see into the water and spot any fish that may be about. There is bound to be a lot of glare, even on quite dull days, so glasses are very important. This is not a good area in which to try and save money. Get the best glasses you can manage. Your optician will have prescription-quality sunglasses at prices that are not exorbitant. A cord attached to the ear pieces, and fitting around your head, will allow you to drop them from your eyes, should you find it helpful to do so. For those who already wear glasses, clip-ons that flip up are available.

A hat with a peak will also serve to keep the glare from your eyes. During the warmer periods, a light hat with as big as brim as you can find will do, bearing in mind that it should also be able to keep your head dry when it rains. Even though the trout fishing season covers the warmer months of the year, there is a considerable part of it that isn't so warm, and can be very cold. In April I have fished in the snow, and once even in May. The guides on my rod froze up and had to be de-iced every so often. April is often a cold month, and sometimes May is, too. It is usually colder and windier on the lake than elsewhere. One year, I recall, I wore a heavy coat through most of the season, including June and July. If it's a question of keeping warm, wear a hat, since up to fifty per cent of your body heat can be lost through your head.

13

Well, never mind the weather. And that's the point. Will you be able to never mind it? If you are properly dressed you can. Remember, you have come fishing for pleasure, and if you are going to be cold or wet, you're going to be miserable, and that is certainly no pleasure. You are going to wind up seeking shelter somewhere, spending your time inside, cowering under somebody's eaves somewhere, or just going home. None of this is necessary if you prepare yourself for the conditions that are almost always prevalent both early and late in the season. You can always take off your coat and sweater if it gets too warm.

Over your normal underwear pull on a pair of long, either wool or thermal, underwear, and put on a long-sleeved shirt in the same material over your vest. You'll keep it cleaner this way, at the same time locking in your body's heat. If you prefer, wear your thermal underwear next to your skin, which may be warmer. Wear a heavy wool shirt over that. If you have a down waistcoat, or can manage to get one, you can put the word *Cold* out of your vocabulary forever more. Down is amongst the warmest things going. And so will you be. To check for quality, feel around carefully; if your fingers discover a lot of stems – those are feathers, not down – try another brand. If you can't manage down, there are synthetics that will do almost as well. There are those who might say – even better. Okay, I won't argue the point – just as long as you can keep warm.

Put a heavy wool cardigan over that, and then put yourself into your warm fishing coat – the one with a hood. A fishing coat without a hood just isn't a fishing coat. Make sure it's rain proof and waterproof – not just water repellent. Waxed coats seem to answer the need fairly well, though they have their disadvantages, too – like, for example, the wax coming off eventually. It will come off faster than it would otherwise when you carry your fishing bag over your shoulder, or rub the sides during the course of rowing a boat. But it can be put back on – and should be gone over from time to time with wax specifically meant for that purpose. Aerosol sprays exist, that you can spray on. The other kind comes in a can – is hard and white. Heat it on a gas or electric ring. It will melt and become the colour of water. Remove the wax from the heat. Paint it on to your coat – which you have hung from a solidly-based wooden hanger – with a paint brush. When the wax begins to harden, heat it up again.

Waxed coats, since they do little by way of breathing, will contribute to the retention of perspiration. If you for some reason become very active, you will find that the lining of your coat is wet. This can be dangerous, particularly if you are then subject to an extreme of cold. Fly fishing, however, is generally not that active. In fact, it is not sufficiently active to keep you warm merely by the effort you exert. Therefore it is necessary to wear enough clothes, and the right ones, to do the job.

That hood will keep the wind off you. You may already be aware of the difference between life with one, and without. There is an enormous difference. Under these cold conditions, a hat, made of waterproof nylon, with a peak, and ear flaps that can be turned down to cover your ears, is ideal.

You will also want to wear a muffler.

Your rubber boots will do little toward contributing to warm feet. Wear two pairs of heavy wool socks – if you can manage to get them, and your feet, in the boot without making it too tight. Most rubber boots, if purchased initially in the proper size, usually provide ample space for extra stockings.

To be warm, you must have warm feet, a warm neck and a warm head.

Fly fishing depends heavily upon hands and fingers. Besides being exposed to the cold, they are also exposed to cold water. Conventional gloves, even those with the fingers out, soon get wet, and are worse than none at all. Hardy does a pair in plastic, with cloth linings, and cuffs that reach high above the wrists. The thumb and index finger are out on both hands; you can manage to cast, to retrieve and to change a fly with movements that are at first a bit clumsy, but improve with practice.

Now, thus prepared, you have banished the misery of cold and rain and sleet and snow. While the others cringe in the lodge, warming their hands over the fire – if there is one – you will be out there fishing. This is why you have come. To spend your time away from the water is sheer waste. You will catch fish only if your fly is in the water, and it will be, only if you keep it there. Don't be frightened off by the cold and rain. Just be prepared for it.

14

Indifferent as you are to the cold, you are prepared to take fish. When that happens, you need a bag in which to hold your fish. In the colder weather keeping them fresh isn't too much of a problem. Later it will be. Many trout fishermen use straw bags. They serve very well. I prefer those made of jute. They last longer; they are easy to clean; they are cheap; and they fold up small – sufficiently so that they can be easily carried in the pocket of a fishing bag.

In warm weather bags of jute or straw will keep your fish cool. You dip it, containing your fish, into the water, and stand it in the shade. When the bag begins to dry, dip it again. The air, passing over the wet bag, will keep the fish cool.

You will also need a "priest" – a bludgeon meant for dispatching your fish quickly with a sharp blow to the head.

If you can manage it, a fishing waistcoat can be useful, with its many pockets. You need one with at least four good-size pockets – big enough to hold your fly box/wallet – and a number of smaller ones.

Also handy is a Swiss knife; the more that it has on it, the better. Mine has everything on it including a magnifying glass and a philips screw-driver, both of which I have used often. Not long ago a man came to me with his reel, from which a screw had come loose. Fixing it for him was no problem.

In my bag I carry a pair of aluminium shears as well as a sheath knife, used for cleaning my fish. If possible, I do this on the spot, after I have finished fishing. I also carry a tube of grease, meant for lubricating my reel, though vaseline will also do the job. A torch, preferably flat, dispos-able or battery-powered, can be invaluable. There is a tube of lip salve, to be applied before starting to fish, protection against wind and sun. I've also got a miniature first-aid kit: antiseptic cream, sticking plasters, aspirin and insect repellent.

Be careful about getting antiseptic cream and such things on your fingers, since they can be rubbed into the fly. While trout do not depend upon their sense of smell to feed – but on their sight – they nevertheless are keenly aware of the smell of strong pharmaceuticals, which will really put them off hitting your fly. I had this happen to me down in Damerham once, using antiseptic cream constantly on the bites that an invading swarm of insects inflicted on me; the fish, on several occasions approached the fly, but turned away suddenly. I wound up the day without taking a single fish.

In a small plastic bag I carry a pair of tiny pliers; a piece of heavy cord; a little sharpening stone – for sharpening my hooks and knife; and a thermometer. The thermometer is attached to fifty feet of line, with knots tied at three-feet intervals. As mentioned before, trout feed at tempera-tures between 50°F and 65°F (water temperature). Therefore, should the situation require it, I'll search for water where these temperature con-ditions exist. I will want to know at what depth so that I can get my fly there. Generally, this is a factor of more importance on a big reservoir where the depths are greater, rather than on a small water.

I have a scale with a tape measure attached; lead shot in various sizes – should there be a need to take my fly down deeper and faster; fullers earth, for rubbing on a leader to make it sink – usually for use with a floating line when the fly is meant to be a short distance below the surface. There is a chemical wax for making the leader float, and a liquid for assisting the fly to float. A cloth or similar, in a plastic bag, is handy for drying your hands, after having handled a fish. This is my list. You may want to add to it – or subtract. Your needs and your requirements will be different from mine, and you are the best one to know and to discover precisely what they are.

15

Hopefully you don't smoke. Hopefully you never will. Smoking and fishing are opposites from each other – in every way – despite the advertisements to the contrary. They try to make it appear that smoking is a part of the sportsman's life – when in fact it is in every way harmful to the sportsman and will serve only to seriously curtail his sport. Don't let yourself be conned. Don't fall into their trap. The price you are forced to pay is enormous.

Earlier we were discussing how to keep warm. None of those things will help the smoker much; he is still going to get cold. The nicotine in the tobacco causes the arteries to contract. This in turn prevents sufficient blood from flowing through them. In the case of extremities – fingers and toes – with blood not reaching them properly, it is impossible to keep them warm. In extreme cases people have lost their limbs because of an insufficiency of blood in the region.

Fly fishing requires the expenditure of an enormous amount of energy over an extended period. The smoker cannot sustain the effort that requires one to stand on a bankside for many hours. He has to quit, at least from time to time, to rest. That means he isn't fishing, and he isn't catching fish.

You have heard about the hazards to health. They are all true. Tobacco is a drug, and like with most drugs, once they've got you – you're hooked. You no longer have a free will. You are compelled to go on using tobacco – compelled to buy it, to put out the kind of money that would otherwise pay for your fishing tackle and for your fishing.

Many young people feel that smoking is an adult kind of thing to do, and certainly the tobacco companies foster this. I have been through this myself, so I am talking from experience, and not second hand. By the time I realized that smoking was neither fun nor grown up – I was hooked, and I couldn't stop. I endured sheer misery for a very long time. For more than a year I worked at stopping. It was the hardest thing I ever tried to do. In the end I succeeded. It is one of my proudest achievements.

Now if you do smoke, how are you going to stop? It's not simple. But it can be done. Pick a time when you are going to have a break in your regular routine – say, the next time you plan on going fishing. Tell yourself that that is when you are going to stop. Think about it. Plan for it. Prepare for it. The idea is that instead of a cigarette, you will reach for something else – boiled sweets, mints, chewing gum – you decide what. When the day comes, when you want a cigarette, have a mint instead. That is what I used – it worked for me; I never thought anything would and I was in pretty bad shape. You suck on the mint, and after you finish, you feel like a cigarette. But you don't have a cigarette. You have another mint. And so it goes on through the day. You will have gone a whole day without a cigarette. When this happened to me, it seemed like a miracle.

You do it the next day, and the next – until one day – you don't want a cigarette. The desire is completely gone. You've kicked it. It took me three weeks. That's about average. You know you have won. It's a marvelous feeling. I went on for some time eating mints – but they're not habit forming – and one day the need for them disappeared, too. You can't ever take another cigarette, because if you do, the chances are good that you'll be back on them again. Pipes and cigars are in no way an improvement over cigarettes, and belong in exactly the same category.

16

In late spring and summer, when the days are long, it is easy to spend twelve or fifteen hours fishing. Such long hours require an enormous expenditure of energy – more perhaps than you realize. I heard about one chap, the friend of a friend, a footballer who had enormous reserves of energy and was in first-class condition. They took him fly fishing for the first time in his life. They fished the whole day, but not for longer than was normal for them. But this poor chap – the footballer – was literally carried back to the car by the others.

To put in those kinds of hours you have to be in good condition. That means eating properly – eating the things that are as close to natural as you can get them, things that are free from chemical additives. Pack yourself a good lunch, something high in protein – cheese, ham, peanut butter. If it is sandwiches, get the darkest, coarsest bread you can find. End with fruit – apples or bananas are nice.

In my bag I also carry emergency rations. It is possible that I stay out longer than I had at first thought I might – that I hadn't yet caught my fish. And I'm hungry, and tired. In my emergency ration bag I've got a block of mint cake. Two or three squares of it and I'm pretty much restored. I also have a bag of granola. At least I'm not going to starve. Torbloken, the Norwegian mountaineers' emergency ration, is a very good thing. While you can fit the whole thing in the palm of your hand, you could probably live on it for the whole of the day if you had to.

17

Fish generally feed more actively in the morning and evening. That is a generalization, not a hard and fast rule. On many occasions I have gone fishless in the morning and taken all my fish mid-day. The fish don't know the rules and aren't going to live by them. However, I like to start as early as I can. It gives me a longer day. If I haven't taken my fish, I'll be there for what everyone hopes will be the evening rise – not that there is any guarantee that one is going to happen. I like to start early so I can say hello to the sun. It's nice being there at the start of day. There is a quietude about it not felt at any other time. Often you are there on your own. The water is yours. For me it's a marvelous feeling.

Some waters don't allow you to start until fairly late; I always feel as if I have missed the best part of the day, though in the end I probably won't have taken any less fish.

If you are getting away early there is no need to disturb the family. They are not going any place and they don't want to be disturbed because you are going fishing. It isn't fair, and in the end, they will become unsympathetic to your fishing, and possibly downright hostile. You are dependent upon the family's good will, and probably, financial help, so don't do anything that will destroy that good will.

Get everything ready the night before – your clothes, your tackle, your lunch, everything you are going to need that day. Upon arising, when it is still dark, you don't want to have to start searching for your clothes and your tackle. Put everything that you are going to need together. Dress somewhere where the light won't bother anybody. Do you have everything? There is only one way to be sure. Make a list. Make a permanent list, something like the one below. And before you leave the house, all you have to do is check it off. That way, you'll never forget anything. If you acquire something new, add it to your list. If you are taking something that will only be taken on this one occasion, write it down on a piece of paper and clip it on to your list. It is extremely difficult to remember the multitude of things that you will require, or might require, on this day, particularly when you are desperately eager to get out.

RODS	✓	✓														
HAT	✓	✓														
NET	✓	✓														
BAG	✓	✓														
SUNGLASSES	✓	✓														
BOOTS	✓	✓														
LUNCH	✓	✓														
THERMOS	✓	✓														
COAT	✓	✓														
NOTEBOOK	✓	✓														
COLD BOX	✓	✓														

The List Card
Here is a suggestion for a list card, though you needn't stick rigidly to it. Make it to suit your own needs and requirements. Use it, and you will never again forget anything.

Allow yourself enough time to eat breakfast, and eat a good one. Some people don't like eating early and may even find it difficult. But once you start in, it seems quite normal and natural, despite the early hour. A good breakfast will set you up for a good start to the day.

What will you be taking along to drink? If it's cold, a thermos of something nice and warm will go down very well.

44

Do you have a notebook with you, and a ball-point pen? You should – to note down the events that occur today – things that are significant at the moment, but that later you might forget. You might want to make a drawing – of a fly, of the lake, of where you caught your fish or where somebody else did.

You will also want to keep a diary – a completely separate volume. This you can fill in when you get home, aided possibly by what you have recorded in your pocket notebook. Why do you want to keep a diary? For two reasons. The first is that you have a permanent and lasting record of your fishing trip – of every one. Each time you read over your diary you can relive that day. It will be a source of pleasure for you for the whole of your life.

The second reason is that it will make you into a better and more knowledgeable fisherman. You will take considerably more fish with it than you will if you don't have one. It will be a reference book, a source of first-hand information that you have produced. You look at it, as a guide book, telling you when, where and how you caught your fish – or failed to do so – on a given date. You will know how to repeat your successes, and avoid any failures.

Get yourself a spiral notebook, one with enough pages to last you the fishing season. The size doesn't matter much – five inches by eight inches or larger will do just fine. This is what you will want to record. It is probably best to write it down on a piece of cardboard the same size as your diary and lay it next to the page on which you are writing.

How much did your fish weigh? And how many of them were there? What fly did you use. You may have used a different fly for each one of your fish. How big was the fly? the hook? What line did you use – if it was a Weight Forward No. 8, slow sink, write that down. What was the breaking strength of your leader, and how long was it? What was the speed of your retrieve when the fish struck your fly? How deep was the fly? How were you casting in relation to the wind – into it, across it, against it? Did you fish from a boat, or from the bank – what was the location when you caught your fish? On which lake did this happen – some fisheries have more than one body of water on which you may fish, so you will want to note this. What was the weather like, and what was the direction of the wind? What was the weather like when you took your fish? At what time did you take your fish? Did you have any hits or follows? Which fly? What was the condition of the water – clear, muddy, weedy, rough? Was the water cold, warm, medium cold? Were the fish rising today? Could you tell on what they were feeding? What other flies were successful today – possibly the people whom you encounter will tell you on what flies they took their fish – or you will ask them. Did you use droppers (more about that later) and if so, on which one did they take? What time did you start fishing, stop fishing.

You will also want a page or two on which you can write any notes that you feel are pertinent – things that you observed – like, fishing at the dam was slow until the wind changed, or something that somebody told you that might be worth noting. Perhaps you will have noted particular forms of aquatic life which you will want to draw, with the eventual purpose in mind of reproducing something similar as a fly. Or perhaps someone will show you a fly that you would like to reproduce, and will, initially, reproduce it into your notebook, then into your diary.

You might also want to make a drawing of the lake you fished, where you fished on it, where it is deep, where it is shallow, where the "hot spots" seem to be. Keep your records faithfully. You may even find it useful to carry your diary with you. But in either event, don't neglect it. Memory has a way of playing tricks on us. Your diary, you will find, will become an increasingly valuable part of your fishing world.

18

Well, let's go fishing. It's spring – and it's cold. You got all your equipment ready the night before. Your lunch is packed, and you haven't forgotten anything, because you've got a list and you checked everything off before you left home.

At the water it's even colder than it was back home. The wind is blowing hard, and there's a sheet of ice along the shoreline. The sky is leaden, and it looks like it's either going to rain or snow. The idea that the sun even exists is difficult to believe at this point. The trees are still bare here, though some of the city trees looked as if they were getting ready for spring. The water is a kind of blue grey. What could possibly be hatching in that? you wonder. On what could the trout be feeding – those that had spent the winter here, and those that have been recently stocked?

It doesn't look like spring, but merely an extension of winter. A lot of people try to get out on opening day, which usually isn't very nice; it's filled with frenzy. Time was when they stocked just prior to the opening, and usually not again until next year. But now most waters stock regularly, some of them, every day, in order to keep up the levels. So it is no longer necessary to be the first. Admittedly, we are all pretty anxious to be out there on the water, rod in hand. It's been a long and hard winter, and this is the day for which we have waited all this time.

You rig up your rod. It's real now. There were times during the winter when you wondered if it was ever going to happen. You pull up your hood against the wind. The cold doesn't bother you – not with that down waistcoat on. It doesn't touch you. If anything, you feel quite warm, as if you were walking around plugged into an electric blanket. There are other people about. They look cold. They are. You can see your own breath.

You feel confident. You know your casting is going to be pretty good – you've been practising on the Common through the winter. Yes, some of those people passing by who saw you really had a field day at your expense – fly-casting on the Common in mid-winter. No, you hadn't caught anything then, but you are certainly going to try now.

There is nothing showing on the water. You don't expect that there will be. The fish are there – down deep, grubbing around on the bottom for whatever they can find.

The wind is coming from the west. You're glad of that at least. An east wind would probably make things even worse. On a lot of waters, the fish react badly to an east wind, particularly if it persists. Not that a north wind is filled with benevolence either. That's the wind that brings the cold – and keeps it. You look at the water. What does it tell you? In the beginning, probably not very much. But as you gain experience, as you come to know a water, it will say things to you, it will speak to you. This will happen without your being conscious of it. If this is your first time on this water you probably feel at something of a loss and rather confused. Don't worry – in time it will all come.

Let's get over to an east bank, maybe find a cove, or some irregularity in the bank's structure. Whatever can be blown over in that direction by way of insect life will be there – not that at this time of year there will be all that much. Here's a place – a smallish cove. Let's start here. With what fly are you going to start? You look through your fly wallet carefully. How about a Black and Peacock Spider. Attach it to your leader – the six-pound stuff – with a blood knot. Make four full turns with it, less than that and you stand a good chance of getting it pulled off the leader. A blood knot is quick to tie, and very strong. If you know a knot you like better, use it. With your scissors around your neck, snip off that excess piece of leader. To see if your fly is tied securely, anchor the bend of the hook through the finger-hole of your scissors, and pull the leader just above the hook. This will serve to tighten the knot as well as to test it.

Considering that the wind is fairly stiff, two feet of leader should be about right. If it's hard to handle, switch over to that ten-pound leader.

Start out fishing across the wind. It's not really difficult. A cross wind assists your line on its outward thrust. Your fly hits the water. It lies there, bobbing on the rough surface, and so too does the new, stiff leader. But the line begins to sink. Get it down. Get it down deep. Don't rush to begin the retrieve. Now at last the line has disappeared. Remember, it is a slow sink line. Give it a chance to get down there.

Now it has. Now begin the retrieve, slowly, in little jerks. That's a splendid beetle you've got there, delicious and delectable. It makes its way over the bottom, back to shore. As you see it at your feet it seems to you to be a living thing. You can hardly believe that anything that looks so real can be just some feathers tied together.

Cast out again. Had it gone down deep enough last time? You are casting well. The line goes out, seemingly without effort. Down it goes. You wait longer this time. Again you retrieve. But still nothing. For how long do you persist? Not too long. As mentioned earlier, trout feed by sight; they are in the business of seeing so that they can spot the food on which they live. They also see colours – pretty much like you do. Not a lot that happens near you is missed by any trout that happen to be in the vicinity. If you, and perhaps others, have gone wading into the water, it is possible that you have scared off the fish. It's better, in all probability, that you don't wade in. But when one does it, everyone else feels compelled to do it, too.

If scaring the fish off isn't the problem, there is no point in persisting with that fly for too long. Perhaps it has been seen and rejected. Perhaps on this water such a creature is alien, and that makes the fish suspicious. There doesn't appear to be any interest. Perhaps you are not casting over fish. On a small water your chances of doing so are fairly good. But on a big reservoir, you can't be sure. Parts of it may well be a vast watery desert. This is why one looks for signs, for some indication that fish are feeding or are otherwise in the area. Sometimes you can see them. But today you can't.

Do you think you're casting over fish? You don't know. Cast out in all directions. Cover the water. No takers. Let's try another fly. What is it going to be this time? What about that Ombudsman. That looks like something that should be crawling about in the mud. It's impossible to say what, specifically. But as often as not you don't have to be too specific. Snip off the Black and Peacock Spider. Attach it to the sheepskin patch you are wearing around your neck. Out goes the Ombudsman. Bring it back slowly. It's right on the bottom. Stop it for a moment altogether. Sometimes that's when they hit it. Or sometimes they hit it when you start moving it again. Maybe there is a big old trout watching it.

Rainbow trout are roamers, almost constantly on the move. If there were a way out of this water, up a river, into another lake, they would be making the trip. Brown trout, on the other hand, don't go any place much. They are territorial. They pick out a place, and that's home. The food that is in their domain – that's theirs – though during some parts of the year they seem to be more concentrated than at others. This may be the case in spring and autumn, when one sees more browns than usual. They are often rather unpredictable; they get stocked, may go to the bottom and never get seen again. Some days your entire bag can be made up of browns.

You're hit! Something has your fly! Hold the line in your left hand. Don't let any slack develop. He runs. Let him take that line out through your fingers, keeping some pressure on it. Your rod is bending. It's a marvelous feeling, isn't it. This is why you have come. This is why you are here. Everything has led up to this moment. Your heart is beating so fast you think it's going to pound right through your down waistcoat. Listen, it always will feel that way. That's what is so wonderful about this game. No matter how many fish you catch, it's always a thrill, as if it were the first time. When it stops happening, that's when you'll stop fishing.

Keep your rod up. You don't have him yet. Don't count him until he's in the net. At any second he can throw that hook. Start bringing back some of that line the first moment he'll let you. He's a big one. We can't see him yet. He's sulking down there, convinced that his sheer bulk will beat you. You manage to get some of the line back. But he makes a sudden dash and he takes back more than he gave.

You're doing fine. The old heart is pounding for all it's worth. Stay

50

calm. This looks like it's going to be a long fight, a hard battle. You've got to play him, play him to the end, tire him out. Take back that line when you can. Somebody somewhere may have told you to play your fish off the reel. Don't! For heaven's sake, don't! You haven't got anywhere near the control that way. With the line running through your fingers, in, or out, you've got the feel of things right at your finger tips. The scream of the reel might sound nice to the ear, but when there's some slack you have to try and gather it up on the reel before your fish takes advantage of the situation and makes his get-away. He might also snap the leader in the process of stripping the line off the reel. It's happened to me.

You're bringing in more line now than he's managing to take back. It's in a fairly big pile at your feet. Be careful you don't stand on it – because if that fish makes a lurch the leader will snap and your fish will be gone. Admittedly that wouldn't happen if you played the fish off the reel, but on balance you're safer this way.

The fish is closer to the surface now. There he is – just for a second – and he's back into the depths again. He is big. Your heart is in your mouth. You want that fish. You want him desperately. Stay calm. You can't horse him in. He won't give you an inch he doesn't have to give. With your right hand index finger hooked around the line, you retrieve that line with your left hand.

That fish is tiring now. But he's not beaten. Not yet. You move him along the surface for several feet, closer to you, and he offers practically no resistance. Then suddenly he shakes himself and fights you, taking back several feet of line. But you're winning. Concentrate on that fish. Don't turn away, don't talk to anybody, don't let your attention wander. Have you got your net ready? It should be near by. Curl your right index finger around the line and hold it against the handle, keeping the pressure on the rod. Reach for your net. Do you think your fish is ready to come in yet? Not your fish – not yet. That fish. That fish on your line.

Hold the net in your left hand. Stoop down low. Put the net in the water, the handle resting on the shore. Bring the fish in closer. He could make another lurch now. You think he's ready? Don't scare him with the net.

Put it under him. Bring him over it. There is still lots of fight left in him. He swims over it. You don't have him yet. He's taken back a yard. He's fighting all the way. Rainbows will, you know. Bring him closer. Many a fish has been lost at the net. Don't lose this one. He'll go three pounds and a bit, easy. Now you've got him close. Move the net under him. That's it. Now scoop him up. He's yours!

You have got him on the bank, enmeshed in your net. The hook has dropped out of his mouth. If you hadn't kept a taut line, that probably would have happened before he reached the net. You breathe a sigh of relief.

Now get your priest. Hold the fish firmly at the gills with your left hand. With the priest in your right hand, deliver a hard blow to the head. The one should dispatch him. If it hasn't, do it again. How do you feel? Wonderful! Of course you do.

Want to weigh your fish? Why not. You've got a scale with you. Let's see what he goes. Three pounds, five ounces. He's in beautiful condition, too.

Somebody comes over to you. It's an older man. You'd seen him fishing some distance away. "Nice fish," he says.

"Thank you," you reply.

"What did you take him on?"

"Ombudsman."

The man nods. Maybe he's been fishing for forty or fifty years, but he's come to you for information.

You feel proud and very pleased. Why not? But for heaven's sake, don't brag and don't boast. Don't say it was easy. Don't say it was a mere nothing. If somebody pays you a compliment, be gracious. This is your moment of glory, your moment of triumph. Enjoy it. They are all too rare. Good sportsmen don't boast, don't swagger. They are always modest. If you have done well it will become known quickly enough; there is no need to tell anyone how good you are. It is a cushion against the time you fall. And fall you will, because everybody does.

This isn't an easy game. It's a hard one. Do you know that at the public reservoirs, the average is something like just over one fish per person per rod. There are smaller, private waters with pretty stiff daily fees that boast of a two fish per rod average. It means, for example, that for the one fisherman who takes a six limit on a public water, there will be five others who will go home without any.

All right, then. What's the limit here? Four? Put your fish in your fish bag and let's see if we can't try for those other three.

19

That Ombudsman did very well for you. Do you think it will work again? Cast it out and let's see. If one fish took it, it seems reasonable enough to expect that another one will, too. Can one assume that this is the kind of thing on which they are feeding today? Well, at least it's a clue, but don't assume anything. What might seem reasonable to you and to me, might not necessarily impress the fish.

You cast out the Ombudsman. You don't really think you're going to get hit in the very next cast, but a part of you says that it can happen. It can. And it sometimes does. But not this time. And not the next time, either. You cast again, and again and again. Your arm is beginning to ache.

They've had plenty of opportunity to see, and reject that fly. What about putting on a Viva? Remember, black is good at this time of year, and so is white. Get it down deep. Be careful you don't get sloppy with your casting, which can easily happen when you start to get tired.

What time is it? You'd forgotten about time – never even bothered to look at your watch. It's past noon. But it seems like you've only just started. That's what happens with those fishing hours – they go by so quickly – that's why they are such precious hours. Don't waste them.

You realize you are also hungry. Let's have some lunch. You find a nice tree that gives you some shelter from the wind – not that you're cold – and unpack your lunch and thermos. There's still plenty of time – don't feel anxious. You can't help feeling a bit anxious, though – and warnings to the contrary won't help you much.

While we're eating, let me tell you what happened to me one day – at lunch time. To be honest with you, I don't really like stopping my fishing to eat, and sometimes I do them together. It isn't a practice I'm recommending, you understand. But that's the way I'm built, and I can't help it, so I'm not fighting it. Sometimes I'll cast out, and while I'm waiting for my line to sink, I'll take a bite of sandwich, and chew it while I retrieve. At other times I'll reel in, and relax for a few minutes over my sandwich.

A lot of people go off mid-day for a couple of hours. They will tell you that it doesn't do any good trying to catch fish then – that it's just a waste of time. Fortunately the fish don't know this. There are times, I admit, when things can go pretty dead, mid-day, though it's no hard and fast rule, which reminds me of another story. But let me get to that first one first.

I was at Black Swan, a lovely lake in Berkshire, now closed. I'd fished the morning, with no outstanding success. Now I was hungry and tired, and the only thing to do for that was to sit down on the bank-side and have my lunch, though I really hated to stop fishing. I rigged up a floating line and greased the leader to make it float, and attached a Dry Sedge to it. I cast it out onto the water, where it floated nicely, and got down to my lunch. I sat on the bank, which was quite steep at that point, my rod nearby, supported by some foliage, and ate leisurely. Occasionally I glanced up at the fly, which gave the appearance of being very real. But apparently, up until this point, if any fish did see it, they weren't much impressed.

I was starting on my second sandwich, and sipping cold milk from the plastic cup that belonged to the flask, when I looked up casually to check on the fly. It wasn't there. Perhaps the wind had carried it off some distance and my eye had not fallen upon it yet. I scanned the area. There was no fly. Could a fish have taken it? Could it have sunk?

Frantically I looked for a place to set down the cup, which, on that steep bank, wasn't easy to find. The logical part of my brain said that there wasn't any need to hurry, because if a fish had been there in the first place, there certainly wasn't one there now. But the part of my brain that ignores anything logical said, What if there is?

I scooped out a level place on the bank where I could put the cup, and grabbed for my rod. Quickly I began retrieving line. Suddenly the line pulled back, and out streaked a fish. I brought him back, and eventually put the net under him. It was a brown trout that went about three-quarters of a pound. It had swallowed the fly. I had not seen him take it, nor heard him, and I had never before known of a trout to actually swallow an artificial fly, though it has no doubt happened before.

Normally, in dry fly fishing, you hold the rod in readiness and keep your eye on the fly, because when the fish strikes it – if he strikes it – you have to let him take the fly under. Then pull – in order to set the hook. If you strike too soon, you jerk the fly right out of his mouth. If you wait too long, he spits the fly out, aware that this isn't anything to eat.

I'm not sure how many fish will swallow your fly, but you will have plenty that will hit it so hard that the hook will become imbedded fairly well down. We'll talk more about dry fly fishing later.

The other story – well, it was at Weir Wood in Sussex, a beautiful reservoir of almost three hundred acres, since closed to trout fishing for no good reason. But, hopefully, by the time you read this, it will be open again for us. I was in a boat, near the dam. The day was hot and bright and sunny, the kind of day a lot of fishermen will tell you you can't catch fish, because trout are supposed to hate the sun. The sun does get in their eyes, and since they have no way of closing them, they're not exactly happy with the sunny weather. But that doesn't mean they stop eating.

A couple of men I'd talked to earlier gave up when the sun was high over head, and made for a darker place. Maybe some people use the bright sun as the excuse for spending the middle of the day at the pub, but I don't know of anybody who ever caught fish in one – at least not trout on a fly. And certainly these men didn't. I stayed and fished – getting down fairly deep. All through the bright part of the day I took fish. When I saw the men later they asked how I had done – I knew how they had done.

"Five," I said.

"When did you get 'em?" they asked.

"Mostly at high noon."

"While it was bright and sunny?"

"That's right."

"Impossible."

In their heads they had it that it couldn't be done, and anything that said otherwise wasn't going to be allowed to penetrate. But those men were far from unique; many people insist that you can't take fish when the sun is shining, despite every evidence to the contrary. So if anybody tells you this, thank them for their help and go on fishing.

20

You've finished lunch, and now you're eager to get back. You don't have to worry about the sun getting in the fish's eyes today. Do you want to go back to the same place? Let's try somewhere else. A change always feels good. You approach it with new hope.

We walk along the bank, looking at the water, at the shore line, for perhaps an indication that there are fish in the area. Sometimes you can see them moving close to the shore. Wading isn't permitted on many waters, which is just as well. A lot of people wading out into the water will often turn the fish away. The ripples you make when wading are telegraphed to wide areas of water, which, for a trout, will spell danger. Keeping to the bank, even when wading is permitted, is often a very good thing.

We move along the bank. There's another fisherman. "How you doing?" he asks. You tell him. How is he doing. He's got one. What did he take it on? A Baby Doll. That's white. Bear it in mind. Asking is a good thing. It will often provide clues, short cuts, that will help you to arrive at the method or methods that will be successful today. You learn the shape, the colour, and you also want to ask about the depth and speed of the retrieve. If it's a nymph-type fly, the retrieve is probably dead slow; at this time of the year, most things are moving dead slow. And they're usually deep down. Newly-introduced fish may be closer to the surface and may be taking a greater variety of flies which may, in fact, have little or nothing to do with what is actually going on in the water.

Here's a place that looks inviting. The wind continues to blow from the west, though not as hard as before. It's warmed up a little; at least the ice around the edges is gone. It's nice to explore a lake, to discover its shoreline, to follow it along as it divides itself from the land. Parts of it will say to you, come and fish here – because it is inviting – because experience tells you that here fish could be lurking. Sometimes you will get it right and sometimes not. There are many factors, few of which you will actually know about, though experience on the water will make it apparent which areas are better during particular times of the year. It is possible that here the lake bottom is conducive to survival of aquatic insects, or shrimps, or other life, on which the trout feeds.

It's a rather jagged stretch here – not deep close to the shore, though it appears to drop off rather sharply a little ways out; the water is somewhat darker. Let's put on the Baby Doll. You cast with it for a time and nothing happens. You go on to the Jack Frost – that's the white marabou, with the red-dyed cock feather at the front. You cast with it for a while, and you start wondering what to put on next. That's when you get hit again. It feels good, doesn't it. You thought it was never going to happen – that the fish in your bag – it was a kind of fluke. Well, there's another one out there, and it's on your line, and one thing is for sure – he doesn't want to stay there. He jumps out of the water and shakes his head furiously, trying to throw that hook. He's a good fish – not as big as the one in your bag – but one you'd certainly like to take home.

He dives. He goes for the bottom, and when that doesn't do him any good, he makes for the surface again. He's out of the water, balancing on his tail, shaking that head. And all you can do is hold on. If the line is too taut, he could snap it. He doesn't. But suddenly your line is slack. Your fish is gone. He's thrown the hook. You feel terrible. Listen, it happens. It happens a lot. That's part of the game and you're going to have to accept it. There are going to be days when you could lose more fish than you actually bring in. This game is filled with disappointments and frustrations. Get used to them; this wasn't the only fish in the lake.

Better check your hook. It could be broken. It isn't. Back it goes. You want a fish so desperately, it hurts. Become accustomed to the feeling. You will suffer from that pain the whole of your fishing life.

But now suddenly there is relief as a trout strikes again. He's on, and you're scared. You don't want to lose this one. They don't come easy. You play him cautiously. He fights hard, but ultimately you bring him in, and you breathe a sigh of relief. He's 1 lb 14 oz, a nice rainbow that fought every inch of the way. You feel marvelous. You have a vision of going home with four fish today. It's not impossible.

That Jack Frost is back in the water. You feel alive, tingling with anticipation and hope and confidence. But then nothing happens. Nothing happens for a long time. Change the fly. What about that White Muddler? It can be good. Your fingers tremble as you cut off the Jack Frost and tie on the White Muddler. The fish are out there, waiting, looking. Is this what they're waiting for? Are you going to wind up with just your two? Don't complain. It wouldn't be a bad day. But if you got a limit – that would mean the best you could do.

The day is passing. Do you still think you can do it? When you don't think you can – you're beaten. Put on the Black Muddler. That doesn't even get a touch. The Whisky – try that. First cast with it – a hit. But there's no fish on. Often it happens on the first or second cast; maybe it's the introduction of something new. Stay with the Whisky – for a while, anyway. Another hit on it. Orange is a good colour – often – not always. Nothing is *always*, not in fly fishing.

What is this Whisky Fly – what does it represent? A "lure" they call it – which means it lures – provokes – isn't a part of the identifiable items trout eat. Did you know you weren't a "purist"? It's bound to come up eventually, so be prepared, and face the fishing facts of life. There are

58

those who will tell you that true sportsmen use only imitative patterns, something that represents real and actual trout grub. Man has given them the designations – as well as the valuations. This is an old argument, and one that will go on forever. You can be sure of one thing though: the chap who was castigating his colleagues for using the Whisky Fly will put one on the first moment somebody takes a fish on it, and his so-called imitative patterns don't earn him so much as a passing glance from a trout.

Right now, though, you've got more than a passing glance – you've got a fish on that fly. He's stripping out line, and that reel is singing. How's the backing – did you put on enough? The old heart is thumping like mad. It's obviously a big one out there. He goes to the bottom and sulks, then takes off and heads out of the water, into the sky. He's much bigger than that first one.

Your hands are shaking, It isn't going to do any good to say Stay Calm. Who can be calm at a moment like this? Concentrate on that fish. Don't talk to anybody. Don't answer any questions. There's time for that when your fish is on the bank – if you ever get him there.

He goes skyward again. That fish is over four pounds. You take back some of that line. He's weakening, but he goes out again and doesn't let you have things all your own way. You get him in closer. He runs again, but not as far this time. He isn't beaten, though; don't for a moment think so. This can be a very dangerous time for you.

You move him toward you. You reach for your net and put it close-by. You bring him closer still. He's almost within netting distance. You become aware that somebody is standing near you. "Can you cope?" the voice says. "Or do you want me to net him for you?"

I always net my own fish. For me it's part of the fishing – the thrill of finally putting a net under my fish. If somebody does it for me, he's taken away part of my pleasure in catching that fish. But it's a personal thing, and a lot of fishermen appreciate having someone net their fish for them.

"Thank you," you reply. "I can cope."

You reach for your net, but the fish finds new life and shoots out. You bring him back slowly, get the net under him, and scoop him up onto the bank. He flops around in the net. But now he is yours – really yours.

"Well done," the man says.

Your heart is still going full speed. You dispatch your fish quickly. The hook was well in him. You're having a job getting it out now; it would be easier if your hands weren't shaking so much.

"Over four pounds," the man says, "maybe four and a half."

You weigh the fish on your scale. 4 lbs 9 oz. What a marvelous fish! You can hardly wait to show your catch to your parents.

"What fly?" the man asks.

You tell him.

He says, "I took one on a Black Chenille this morning, but I haven't had a touch since. This your first fish?"

"Third."

He's obviously impressed.

He returns to his fishing. You rinse out your net and leave it on the bank near you. How do you feel now? Top of the world. Of course you do. You keep looking at your fish. It's a monster, isn't it! Your parents are going to be in for a surprise.

You move a short way up the bank. Don't get too far away from your net – that's often when you need it. If you should get a fish on, and your net is some distance away, hopefully there will be someone relatively close by who will assist you. If there isn't anyone, walk your fish along the bank to where your net is, but do it slowly and cautiously. By the same token, if you should see anyone who might be in need of help, be quick to offer your services, just as this man did for you. Some people like help in landing their fish. Later in the season, when the bank is covered with foliage, and there is weed close in, landing a fish can be pretty tricky. If you should ever be doing it for anybody, be particularly careful; you don't want to be responsible for losing a fish for somebody. Submerge the net and let the chap manoeuvre the fish over it, if possible, and then scoop it up.

Well, the day isn't over yet, and you could still wind up with that fourth fish. You carry on casting. Nothing happens for a time. Then you get a hit. The fish is on, and you think you've got it made. Then it's off. They often

60

slip the hook like that. Never mind, keep trying. You do. But nothing happens. Maybe that fly is suffering from over-exposure. Time to put on something else. What shall it be this time? How about the Orange Muddler. They seem to like orange, unless it suggests danger to them by now. Try it and see. You can always take it off again.

Let it sink down. The muddler head is buoyant and tends to make the fly ride high. Bring it in in fits and jerks. If that doesn't work, speed it up. A lot of people do a figure of eight with the line. Stop it altogether, then start again, bring it in a couple of slow feet, and stop it for a moment. Vary your retrieve. The presentation is as important as the fly.

Nothing doing with that Orange Muddler? What do you say we try the Black Muddler. You know, I've often done pretty well with muddlers – at times – not all the time. It was created by an American fly tier for use on a Canadian river, and meant to imitate the fresh water sculpin, which means it does some of its best work riding low and slow in the water, retrieved in erratic jerks.

It's getting colder now, and the not very good light that we've had throughout the day is even less good. It looks as if ice is beginning to form close to the shore. It's going to be another cold night. It could be that the trout have become rather sluggish, and not much interested in feeding; their metabolism has decreased. Maybe you can do some good with that Black Zulu. Under these conditions, you want to use smallish flies.

Dark flies show up better in the water when the light is bad. On dark days, dark flies; on bright days, light flies, is supposed to be the rule. But I've heard of people who have switched it around – and did very well. Bear it in mind, but don't live by it.

The day finally comes to an end. It's been a good day. A limit would have been nice, but if you check around, you'll probably find that there weren't many limits taken today. You're well up there, close to the top. It is nice to take a limit; don't be ashamed of wanting to. It means you couldn't have done better – and that's good. It means you bet on yourself and won.

21

Mum and Dad are delighted. Dad had been rather sceptical. He didn't think he'd be eating trout – except possibly for the little hatchery-raised tiddlers they sell in the supermarket. As a matter of fact, he has never seen such a big trout in his life. Tell them how you did it.

Your Mum, naturally enough, takes your success for granted, knowing all the time that you would do it. Don't let her take your success as a matter of course, and don't you make that mistake, either. Every fishing day is a new battle, and some of them you win ... and the others ... well, you know. But this is your victory, so enjoy it. Dad keeps saying, "I didn't know trout came this big." And then he says, "You know something, I wouldn't mind having a go myself one day – if I thought I could catch trout like that."

Perhaps you will have made your Dad into a trout fisherman. I have known of more than one case where the son has made the father into a fly fisherman, rather than the other way around. If it happens, it's nice. If father and son can share their fishing, it creates a marvelous bond, a closeness that is rarely ever achieved in other ways. It will last a life-time and be forever more a source of satisfaction to all concerned.

You got the fish – you've also got the job of cleaning them. Don't give them to Mum to clean. If you do, there is going to be a lot less enthusiasm around the house for your fishing. Cleaning the fish is the other part of catching them. I, in all truth, wouldn't want anybody else to clean my fish – they're mine and I want to look after them. It's better if you can clean your fish where you have caught them, but that doesn't always work out, so you have to do it at home. It isn't really an unpleasant job and don't think of it as unpleasant, but rather as the continuation of your successful day. Far worse than coming home with fish to clean is coming home without any. You will soon get used to cleaning fish – hopefully there will be plenty for you to clean – and you will do it quickly and efficiently and not give it a second thought. Since it can be a somewhat messy business, it is very important that you neither make a mess nor leave one behind you.

Let's clean our fish. If you don't have Snips, a kitchen scissors will do. Cut forward from the vent. I always cut off the heads; it isn't traditional, and if you don't want to do it, don't. Avoid cutting the intestines, which will help to make the job less messy. Take out the innards. There will be a layer of corrugated blood running the length of the spine. Cut it out with your Snips or scissors. With your knife, scrape away any blood that remains. Rinse the cavity. Avoid excess soaking of your fish, since it absorbs water, and that isn't good. If the skin is eaten, scale the fish. Put it in a colander while you get on with your other fish.

When that job is done, dry the fish with kitchen paper, both inside and out. You can also use ordinary paper bags for the job, which are cheaper. If fish are not to be eaten immediately, storing them in the freezer – if you have one – is the best solution. Use a thick polythene bag, meant for freezing food, sucking the air out of it, and sealing it tightly. Cling-film is also good. Use a double thickness, and seal by touching it to a hot iron that you have covered in advance with a sheet of aluminium foil – meant to keep the cling-film from sticking to the iron.

Attach an adhesive label to the fish, with a number, starting at "1", and going on from there with each new fish that you add. In a notebook meant for recording what's in your freezer, put down the date your fish were caught, and the weight opposite the number. Trout, we are told, should be eaten within six months of freezing, though I have kept them longer, without, apparently, loss of flavour or any other problems, providing they have been properly packed. When you take a fish out of the freezer, defrost it slowly in the fridge. And remember to scratch it off in your book. That way you know just what you've got.

If you don't have a freezer, you can still preserve your fish by salting them. We'll tell you how to do that later on. I don't know exactly what you're planning, but it may very well be a fish dinner, and maybe you'll be inviting some friends or relatives to share it. Why not? It's a real victory celebration, and you have provided it. This is the natural conclusion to your successful pursuit – to bring home your catch and eat it – to share it out amongst those whom you want close to you.

You might even be giving away some of your catch. Don't be casual about it. It is valuable. Make sure it goes to those who appreciate its value. But one thing you must never do – and that is sell your fish. The moment you do that you stop being a sportsman and become a fish-monger. It changes your whole attitude and approach to your fishing.

It is possible that your parents will want to help and encourage you with your fishing; their financial contribution may be essential. But do not accept payment directly, even from them, for your fish. Let them pay for your day of fishing – but not for your fish. However, this concept does not apply outside of home and family; if you let strangers pay for your day's fishing, you have in effect sold them your fish. One can argue the fine points of this, but I am not going to. Just remember, it is your catch. It represents the sum total of your success, of your skill and your ability. Hold all of those things in high regard. Give it the importance it deserves. You pay your kill the highest possible respect when you consume it, when you give it willingly to those who are close to you.

Take special care in disposing of the innards, particularly if it will be any amount of time before the dustmen come to call. You'll find that your dust bin is very popular as a cat rendezvous, and if you have plastic bags as containers, cats can easily claw their way in, even through the quite small mesh of the cage stands used by many councils.

How is your cooking? You may not be highly experienced, but why not cook your catch for the family. As you may already know, trout is not only a wonderful fish to catch, but a magnificent one to eat. Don't take the attitude that cooking is "woman's work", and deny yourself the fun that it can be. Do you think you can prepare dinner for the family? Why not! Let's have a go. One of my favourite recipes is Trout Meunier. It's a bit tricky – you have to be careful with the timing, but it is absolutely

64

delicious; just talking to you about it now makes my mouth water. If you're serving the big fish, you will want to cut them the long way, and then in half, unless you happen to have an exceptionally big frying pan. How to do it follows below. Enjoy it, and good appetite.

Recipe: Trout Meunier

Trout
Approx 4 – 6 oz butter
Salt, pepper/flour (if desired)
2 oz flaked almonds (if desired)
chopped parsley

Season trout with salt and pepper. If desired, roll trout in flour, as well. Heat butter. Using moderate heat, fry trout in butter. Cook for about 30 seconds, then carefully turn trout over. Continue cooking, turning fish occasionally to ensure fish is fully cooked. Be careful not to overcook.

If desired, lightly cook 2 oz flaked almonds in butter in another pan, until golden brown. Take fish out of butter and put on serving dish. Add juice of half a lemon to butter in pan and pour over fish. Finish by pouring flaked cooked almonds over fish and sprinkle with chopped parsley.

22

You can hardly wait to get back out on the water again. Maybe you have even bought some more flies, gone to the shop and carefully selected some patterns that look good to you, and that's fine. Make your own choice, your own decisions, because that is the way you are going to learn. That day out wasn't cheap, but you have been saving your money, going without those chocolate bars, and probably a lot of other things that you would like and would ordinarily buy. But now you've got something really important that requires your money.

Your parents have probably been helpful, and now the big day is here. You learned a lot, and feel pretty confident. Maybe this time you'll be going home with a limit. You get out there as early as you can, fish the flies that brought success last time, maybe get broken on a Baby Doll, and wind up trying every fly in the box. At the end of the day, you haven't caught a thing. You feel shattered – absolutely devastated. Why not? It's perfectly natural. You put all your hopes and aspirations into this day – and then it ended in defeat. You feel so frustrated you could almost go off somewhere and cry. Choose your spot carefully, because you might find somebody already there, crying with frustration.

This won't be the last time either that this will happen. It's part of fishing. You will never get used to it. Don't. Don't accept defeat casually, as a matter of course. The more you know, the more you understand, the less often it is going to happen. Remember, each time you go fishing, the conditions are going to be different. Each new day for you will have its own secret, and your problem will be finding out what it is. The secret may be the fly, the colour, the way you present it, the depth, or any combination.

I often tie flies based on the experience I have had on the water on the day I fished it. But a week later, those flies might be completely useless, since the conditions have completely changed, even in so short a time.

23

Fishing at the publicly-owned waters is usually cheaper than those that are privately owned, but the fish may be smaller. Big fish are nice to catch, but so are small ones. Given the choice, I would sooner catch five one-pound fish than one five-pounder. Many people with whom I have spoken said they would prefer it the other way. I'd rather keep busy catching fish – even if they are smaller.

On some of the private waters you are limited to just one fly on your line. But the public reservoirs allow up to three, and are not concerned either about the size of the hook or the overall size of the fly. Is there any advantage to using more than one fly? There can be, and many fishermen use two or three as a matter of course. The problem for many, particularly those new to fly fishing, is that there are frequent tangles.

The advantages are: your flies are at varying depths; you present a choice of fly. It can be very useful when you have no idea what the fish are taking. It may also start fish feeding, by creating the impression that food is available in abundance. I don't know that this is a fact, though it is claimed by many to be so. However, don't start using more than one fly on your line until you feel you are ready, because otherwise it will only add to your frustration. How will you know when you are ready? If you can use them, and you can cope – then you are ready.

If I get a tangle, and it looks like it might be a bad one, I cut the leader off and replace it with another one. Don't waste fishing time undoing knots. Tie up your own dropper leaders (if and when you start using them) and have a supply of them available as required. The droppers themselves should be kept short, not much over an inch, which will reduce the possibility of tangling. Here is how you tie them:

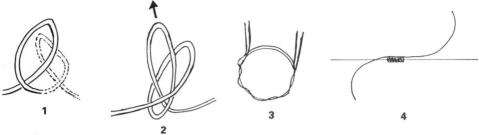

The Dropper Knot

A little practice with this one, and you will soon have it down perfectly.

You want a piece of monofilament about 8 – 10 inches long, which you lay on top of the leader. Create a loop several inches from the end of the monofilament. Create another loop, just to the right of it, as in the dotted line of Figure 1.

Draw it through as in Figure 2.

Repeat that process three more times, which will appear as in Figure 3.

Draw the ends together, as in Figure 4, and trim off the tail.

I tie mine about five feet long, in both six and ten-pound breaking strength leader, with the droppers and point about a foot apart. If you change flies often, as I do, the leader holding the dropper fly is too short to tie a fly on a second time. So I use Mustad Snap Hooks, available in some fishing tackle shops. You tie these on to the dropper leaders, and then slide the flies on and off as required. They work pretty well, though it isn't smooth sailing all the way since the leader sometimes gets caught in the snap hook. The other possibility is to tie your flies onto the dropper and leave them on permanently. When you want to change flies, change the whole leader. Don't forget to leave your dropper leaders sufficiently long to attach the fly in the first place. I find that the best way of carrying these dropper leaders, either with or without the flies attached, is on a cast carrier.

The Cast Carrier

You can make your own out of cardboard, which won't last as long, particularly if they get wet. The plastic ones that you can buy are cheap and last indefinitely.

68

When you dispose of that leader, be sure to cut it up into small pieces so that it will not present a danger to birds who can become tangled up in it. In general, make it a point not to litter, which makes our surroundings ugly. Carry a litter bag with you – a plastic bag will do nicely – and use it for disposing of the things you do not want. A chocolate wrapper is nice on a bar of chocolate, but thrown on the bank side, or on the water, it is an offense to the eyes and to the spirit of the outdoors.

24

Let's have a look at the changing season. As mentioned earlier, at the beginning of the season the fish are usually down deep, scrounging around, and smaller flies, in both black and white can do pretty well, and so can orange. On some waters where the newly-stocked fish have been recently introduced, you can sometimes take fish along the perimeters, not far beneath the surface.

April can be a pretty unreliable month, with some very changeable weather. That east wind isn't anybody's friend, and if it persists for any length of time, it can really become the enemy, though some waters are more adversely affected than others. I don't know the reason for this, and I haven't spoken to anybody who does. Now down at Avington last spring that east wind persisted for a long time – it went on for a couple of weeks, which resulted in some pretty hard going. Fishery Manager Roy Ward said that he had been suffering with a perpetual headache during that period, and that even the fish in the stock ponds had gone off their food. The barometer had been down, and stayed that way; general atmospheric conditions were probably responsible for Roy's perpetual headache. This could be read in terms of a low barometer, and expressed by the constant east wind. Some people are more affected by it than others, and apparently, some fish in some lakes.

By May things are usually starting to warm up, and the nymphs are about in increasing numbers. Trout are also taking winged flies now, and generally not far below the surface. Orange flies often do well, retrieved in rather quick jerks, just below the surface. Spring is often a good time for encountering brown trout. You could pick up a limit of them and not even see a rainbow. A lot of people get pretty enthusiastic about brown trout. They can sometimes be seen feeding on or close to the surface. If you drop a nice gaudy fly where they just happen to be, not far below the surface, you may do well. They are not fish that school together generally, except on occasion in early spring. They are territorial. That is, they stake out their territory and live off of what they find in it. Rainbows on the other hand are always on the move. You may not see browns much again until the autumn.

By June the water is usually fairly warm, the trout's metabolism is high, and there is plenty around to eat. There are often some good evening rises. On some waters the Mayfly is doing well, and where they are hatching, sometimes the trout will concentrate on them, to the exclusion of almost everything else.

If you can manage to get yourself a floating line – do. Having one can be an advantage, particularly for that evening rise. Another line also means another reel, since you can't very well strip off the original line, and replace it with the floater, and then switch back again. Until you can get yourself a second rod – you'll have to switch reels back and forth as required.

I remember one day at Latimer, in Buckinghamshire, when the trout were feeding just beneath the surface, and a floating line was right – until the sky went black, and the fish went down into the depths. When the sky brightened again, in a relatively short time, the fish were back up, and feeding near the surface. Then, in a little while, the sky turned dark, and down went the fish again. I switched rods to accommodate each change. Admittedly these conditions were not typical, but changing over from one to the other and back again in the course of a day can easily happen.

70

July is the time for sedges; your Invicta is one of them, and that can be a very effective fly. They're taking sedges in all the stages of development: larva, pupa, winged adults. They are often rather selective now, and until you get it right, a lot of your other flies will probably be ignored. They become preoccupied with a particular insect and ignore everything else.

Speaking of the evening rise, a lot of people put their faith in it – and go home without any fish. For one thing, it might never happen. The conditions have to be right for it; the insects need to be hatching, and if the evening turns cool they might not be. And even when there is a hatch, you'll be surprised how often it won't do you a bit of good. I have seen this happen many times; so has every other fisherman, and so will you. Even if what they are taking is identifiable, to duplicate it with an artificial does not necessarily bring results. Many has been the perfect evening at Weir Wood when the water boiled with rising fish – none of which I could take on a fly, nor did I see anybody else take any fish. It got to the point where when that boil started, I knew that for me it was time to go home.

Also there to frustrate you is the caneis, known as the "angler's curse". They are tiny white things that come like a snow storm, will get into your eyes and nose, and of course the water, where the trout will shovel them up like they were swimming bulldozers. People have been known to catch fish when the caneis were falling, but not often. You run a fly through the surface of the water – any fly will do – and hope that in the frenzy a trout will grab onto it. This, however, has never happened to me, so I don't want to create any false hopes.

It's not that I want to knock the evening rise. It can certainly save an otherwise bad day. At Latimer on a day in late spring I'd taken only one fish by evening, and it looked to me like that was the only fish I'd be taking home. Then the fish came on to feed in earnest. They were selective, but serious, and green nymphs got me two by the time the light was going. Then a black seal nymph accounted for the limit fish by the time it was getting too dark to change flies.

I'm not really happy about flogging away the last hour or so, desperately trying to get a fish, or another fish. I don't like fishing under pressure, or doing anything else under pressure, for that matter. It puts an undue strain on me, and it will on you as well. It takes the pleasure out of it and makes it work – unpleasant work.

August is, as they say, a wicked month. You never really know what to expect, even to a lesser extent than during the other months. Sometimes it's easy, and sometimes it's very tough. On occasion you can take a limit pretty smartly by skimming a brightly-coloured fly over the surface of the water – you can use your slow-sinking line to do this – but next time they won't chase anything. If it's very hot for an extended period, that will affect their metabolism, and they'll go off their food again, like they do in winter, only now they will have reduced intake while surrounded by abundance.

Greenish flies, nymphs, can sometimes go down well. If they're not feeding on the top, try the bottom. That one man enjoys success on a particular fly is no guarantee that anybody else will find it successful. August can be filled with frustration.

A lot of fishermen are relieved when September comes around, though it can also offer its fair share of frustration and inconsistency. The weather can be changeable, and the first part of the month may be very different from the last part. The trout start devouring fry, which earlier may have been ignored. At King's Langley, a new water up in Hertfordshire, the fish stuffed themselves on fry, which they herded along the edge, and then ploughed into them. I had never before seen such preoccupation with fry – to the exclusion of all else. The limits had been many in earlier days, but then the fish, having gorged themselves, rested, with only two rainbows coming out of the water during the course of a whole day. Such is the way of fish and fishing.

They will still be taking fry in October. If it's a warm day things suddenly begin hatching. Black and white are good colours again. You have to keep trying, keep experimenting, chopping and changing. There might be not just one answer, but several. Check around to see what others are doing. October can also be wicked, and you know that the chances of it getting any better before spring are slim. One day it can really blow up, and then turn warm and mild. At Avington at the end of October, following an early morning frost, it turned into shirt-sleeve weather, and the midges suddenly reappeared, feeding in the area of perspiration around my hat. Sure, I had repellent with me, but who thinks about using it at the end of October?

At Barn Elms in London the fly that got all the action on a cold day in October was one with a black body and orange wing that had been sitting in my box for the past couple of seasons, unused. For some time past there hadn't been the slightest interest shown in it.

There are some waters that stay open in November, and there are also some nice days – though not many. There aren't many hours of light. The last time I fished in November I had to de-ice the guides on my rod. And I didn't catch anything, either. Only one brown trout was taken, and that had to be returned, because the season on brown trout was closed. (Rainbow trout, as an introduced fish, has not had seasons established on it, except by water authorities and private individuals controlling the water.) There are even those waters that fish through Christmas. It's really a very good idea, though you probably won't be meeting me on the bankside. It isn't the cold that worries me, but just that it feels unnatural to me to be trout fishing in winter.

25

I regard contests as another form of payment, and organized competitions as contrary to the best interests of fishing and fishermen. If you have caught a big fish, it is nice to get some recognition. You are pleased, and well you should be. But you really don't need further payment; you have had the immense satisfaction that taking a big fish provides. And if you get your name in the fishing magazines, your achievement has been noted for all to see.

Compete with the fish, not with the fishermen. There is a tendency to organize competitions for many things; perhaps the need for individuals to triumph, or attempt to triumph, over other individuals is very great. But fly fishing doesn't need that kind of competition or that kind of victory. To triumph over a trout is truly a great victory; to make him fall for your deception is a splendid achievement.

If you are wading, besides trying to avoid stomping around noisily, be careful. Lake bottoms have a way of being pretty tricky places. There are rocks on which you can slip, and holes into which you can sink. If you go down, you can ruin your day's fishing; if it's a cold day, standing around in wet clothes won't be very much fun. And it can be dangerous. If you become chilled, with your body temperature substantially reduced, and no longer able to combat the cold, you could be in trouble. Run. Jump. Do something physical to raise your body temperature. If this doesn't work, seek shelter, get out of your wet clothes, and – if they are available – into something dry. And get close to something warm. It is essential that you raise your body temperature.

A wading staff, or even a walking stick, can be a big help if you are wading. You can tie a string around the walking stick and put it over your shoulder while you are fishing, or push it into the bottom and let it stand upright. Moving through the water is difficult in waders, but a walking stick is like a third leg, and will make the going very much easier.

At Grafham Water, in Cambridgeshire, I was walking along the dam, when, putting on my sun glasses, I dropped the glass case. Stooping down to pick it up, I slipped, and fell into the water. It was early spring, and fairly cold. The water seeped into my boots. I was lying flat, with the bottom half of me immersed. I couldn't scramble out because of the slimey rocks. Only by putting my index finger in the seams between the rock facings was I able to pull myself forward. Climbing the cement, which was virtually flat, fighting for traction with arms and legs, I managed eventually to pull myself out.

I emptied my boots, wrung out my stockings, and carried on. My body temperature had not been substantially reduced; probably the physical effort of trying to rescue myself had sustained that heat. Now, walking briskly along raised it further still. My feet remained wet, though reasonably warm, the whole day. But I never so much as suffered from a sniffle as a result of my encounter in the water.

If, after a hard day's fishing, it's still going to take some time and effort getting home, stop to have a cup of tea and something to eat first. You may not even be aware of the extent to which you had consumed your energy and body reserves. Consequently, you may not realize how tired you actually are. You may very well have been up since early morning; by evening you've got to be tired, and your faculties somewhat dimmed.

And one more thing – if your boots are muddy, getting into a car with them isn't going to make you popular. The best way to cope is to put them in a big plastic bag, and do your car riding in normal street shoes.

26

Let's talk about boat fishing. It's a nice way to fish. Whether it's better, is open to debate. But there's no question that it gives you access to water that you could not reach from the bank. Sometimes this can be important; sometimes this can be virtually the only way to catch fish.

But there is the additional cost of the boat, which on some waters is substantial. Sharing a boat may reduce the cost, and in the Anglian Region, which includes Grafham Water and Rutland, double or triple occupancy is the rule. (This is a misguided safety measure that presumes there is less danger to the individual when accompanied by others. Because I fell into the water from their dam doesn't mean I'm advocating the removal of all dams.)

As a matter of fact, sharing a boat has its dangers – both to you and to your partner(s). That fly you are casting is travelling through space at a hundred miles an hour. If it winds up in skin, it's going to do damage. If it goes in beyond the barb, it's best to have a doctor remove it. The victim will need a tetanus injection, penicillin, and, very likely, a pain killer – for the actual removal. It's really a good idea to have yourself inocculated against tetanus before the need should ever arise, and hope that it never does, and then you know you are safe.

It is also possible to hook yourself, particularly if there is a strong wind – one blowing from right to left. Assuming that you are right-handed, the wind may blow the line back over you. Always be conscious of this. Turn, if you can, to fish into the wind, or across it, a method applicable to boat or bank. Co-ordinate your casting with your boat partner so that you don't get in each other's way. With a little practice, you will become fairly competent. But keep your glasses on and your collar up.

Anchor near the dam, assuming that there is one. The chances are, it will be a pretty good place, particularly if the wind is blowing onto it. The dam traps a lot of things fish eat. Put yourself in a position where you can cast in all directions. Back a little ways from the dam, at the centre, is usually the deepest place in the lake. Here the water will be the coolest, which in the warmer weather, will provide the most comfortable place for the trout. Let your fly sink down; give it plenty of time before you begin your retrieve. You have to work at finding the fish, and some days it is harder than others. The area close to either shore, in the vicinity of the dam, can sometimes be very productive.

Speaking of anchoring, not all waters supply anchors with their boats. You have to bring your own. Even where one is available, some people like to use two anchors, one at either end of the boat. That way the boat remains completely steady on the water. It is rather a nuisance to have the boat continually swinging around. If you are going to do any amount of boat fishing, you might want to acquire your own anchor. I have one that weighs just a couple of pounds, with four prongs that fold onto the stem when not in use, but can be opened up like an umbrella when required. The concept here is that the anchor will move along the bottom until one of its prongs bites into the bottom and holds the boat firmly. It is basically a very good concept, and often it works very well. But it does not always work, particularly if the wind is strong.

Attach six feet of chain to your anchor. And to that add stout plastic cord or rope in sufficient length to allow you to fish the deepest part of the lake. There are waters that are eighty or ninety feet deep. You can make your own anchor, using a paint can, filling it with rocks, then pouring in some ready-mix cement. It's a nuisance carrying it around – I know a chap who carries two of them when he goes boat fishing – but they are effective.

Another boat technique is to fish the shore line. That is, casting toward the shore. If you are on your own, you remain seated in the rowing seat, casting toward the bank, and manoeuvring the boat with your oars between casts. Keep yourself parallel with the shore. Constantly on the move, you cover a lot of water, and consequently a lot of fish. Be careful not to interfere with those fishing from shore; you have considerably wider scope and range than they do, so don't muscle in on their territory. If there are two of you in the boat, it is possible for one to row while the other casts, taking alternate stints at the oars.

Seated in your boat, you should be able to cast as far as if you were standing, once you get used to doing so. Since it is arm and wrist motion that sends the fly out into the water, whether you sit or stand shouldn't make that much difference. If you are going to do any appreciable amount of sitting, a boat pillow will be useful, preferably an inflatable one that fits nicely into your fishing bag. Get the kind that is square-ish. It stays on the seat better and is more comfortable for sitting.

If you've got thigh waders on, turn them down while you are in the boat, as a safety precaution. Should you go over, they won't fill up to the same extent were they pulled up full length. You are probably in less danger fishing from a boat than you are wading along the shore. The boats provided on public waters are usually very safe and sturdy. But you should know how to swim. If you don't already know – learn! Don't delay. Do it starting now. The chances are you will never have to do it out of necessity – but at least you won't be afraid that you might. It will go a long way toward eliminating any anxiety or fears. You will know in your heart, that if anything happens, you can look after yourself. It gives you a marvelous feeling of confidence, and when you're fishing, that's what you need more than anything else. That boat pillow can also be used as a life preserver if ever the need should arise. You may also want to consider the possibility of wearing a life jacket, though it's much better to know how to swim.

That you fish with confidence is an absolute necessity. You must feel that everything you are doing is right – your casting, your fly, your position on the water. When that confidence is reduced, then you know it is time to change something.

Another technique when fishing from a boat is to anchor in or near a weed bed. Through holes in the weeds – or if there aren't any, then as close as you can get – let down one or more nymphs. Bring them up in jerks, a few inches at the time. Allow them to drop back several inches, then

Sid fishing from a boat, loch style. The boat goes where the water takes it.

continue the upward climb, repeating until your nymphs have fully emerged.

When casting, bring your flies right back to the boat or bank. It is possible that they have been followed, and the hit will come only at the last second. Always be prepared for it. Suddenly from the depths a fish will emerge, chasing hard after that fly. Stop it to let him take. If the interest disappears, move it slowly and jerkily.

Toward the end of the retrieve, let your fly, if it is one, or the top dropper, if more than one, skim the surface of the water. This could bring on a strike.

A fly pulled quickly, sometimes erratically, over the surface, can also be effective at times, from the bank as well as a boat.

One of the nicest ways of boat fishing, when the time is right, is "loch-style". You have to be on a water that is big enough to allow you to drift where the wind takes you and not interfere with anybody else. It also entails a lot of rowing, all of it against the wind. You start at the point from which you want to drift, manoeuvring your boat, in so far as you are able, so that it drifts broadside of the current. This will make the drift slower than if the prow were forward.

If you are going to do any amount of this type of fishing, it might pay to invest in a drogue. It works on the same principle as a parachute, except that it is pulled through the water, and is meant to slow down your drift.

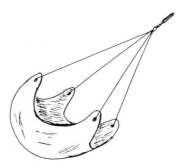

The Drogue
Useful, if you are going to do a lot of boat fishing.

Cast a short line ahead of the boat. One fly is less apt to tangle than two or more, though in traditional Scottish loch-style fishing, a whole bank of flies are used. If there is a tangle, it is better to shove out your anchor and stop your boat long enough to undo it, or you will have drifted across to the opposite bank and will have to row back again and start all over again.

Bring the fly back over the surface of the water. Cast out immediately on that short line, not bothering to false cast. If you get a fish on, drop out the anchor while you play it. For this method to be successful, the fish have to be feeding fairly close to the top, when the hatches are coming off the surface, usually well into the season. It is a method that will work when perhaps all others fail. Flies with silver bodies are often effective, usually fairly small. But here, as with the rest of fly fishing, you have to experiment, keep trying and changing until you get it right. Don't worry about moving the fly through or over the water too fast; a trout after a fly can almost always swim faster than you can retrieve.

27

As the season advances, the fish are often to be seen feeding on or near the surface. But again, waters differ and so do conditions. If you want to fish with a dry fly – a fly that floats – you will need a floating line. Grease your leader with a chemical wax, and dip your fly into a liquid for assisting the fly to float. Cast it out and wait. Twitch it occasionally. If nothing happens, repeat the process. If you get a take, you are going to need courage as well as nerves of steel, since you dare not strike until the fish has actually taken your fly under. There are many misses before there is actually a connection; not all the fish are going to oblige like that brown trout did.

If you want to remove the grease from your leader, rub it with mud or you can buy fuller's earth at the chemist. In powder form, you get it wet, roll it into a ball, and keep it with you in a small plastic container. You can also apply fuller's earth to a leader that you want to sink – when, for example, using a nymph or other fly on a floating line – if you want it to travel just below the surface.

With a midge pupa, grease your leader to within a couple of inches of the fly. This can be more or less, depending upon the level at which you think the fish are feeding. You then watch the line. If it moves, strike! With this method of fishing the takes are often barely perceptible, since nymphs move slowly enough for trout to merely suck them up in passing. I find it extremely difficult to keep my eyes fixed on a piece of line in order to try and detect any movement. Personally I like to fish by feel as well as by sight. For me, the take which I can feel is the most exciting thing there is in fishing. However, don't let me put you off this method if you think you might enjoy it. To make it a little easier, tie a piece of brightly-coloured wool around the line above the point where it meets the leader. It will be easier to watch than the unbroken length of line, which may be obscured by the ripple of the water.

Another version of this is to attach your nymph to the point of the leader, with a floating fly on the dropper, which will serve as a float for the nymph, and will also become a visual alarm for when a trout hits the nymph.

You can also reverse this by putting the floating fly – something fairly big and highly visible – on the point. About four feet up the leader, attach a nymph to your dropper, which will ride head up. You will know when it has been taken by the sudden disappearance of your floating fly, which again serves as a float. It is also possible that your floating fly will be grabbed.

Nymph on Point

A muddler, or other good floating fly, will serve as a float and let you know when your nymph has been taken.

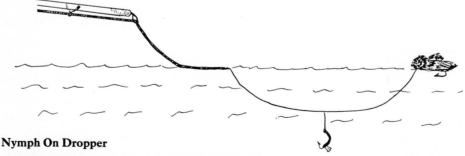

Nymph On Dropper

Reversing the arrangement, with the nymph on the dropper, you can keep it fairly high in the water, with the floating fly on the point.

82

Another sometimes effective technique is to attach three flies to your leader, which you grease, but not the droppers. Cast out, and retrieve slowly, in erratic movements. This is sometimes especially effective around weed beds. Gold bodied flies are recommended.

Stripping your fly back for all you are worth, whether on a sinking or floating line, can also be effective, provoking the kind of smash that is a joy to experience. It does draw scorn from some people, for no really good reason, but if it works at a particular time and place, then use it with great pleasure. It is a method with no less virtue than that of the slow retrieve, which is of use only if effective.

Casting at fish that are visible in water that is clear – such as Avington or Damerham – is another technique. With a weighted fly, you select a quarry – at a place like Avington you select a big one – and cast at it. This stalking method sometimes works very well. A pair of polaroid sunglasses is essential equipment, which will enable you to see into the water.

The sink and draw method, as the name implies, is one where you allow your fly to sink, to whatever depth your own judgement tells you is most effective. You then draw it along, for a foot or so, then stop it and let it sink, repeating the process until the fly has been retrieved.

There will be times when fish will "take short" – hit your fly but not actually get themselves hooked. Sometimes this will occur with an object that provokes them. Sometimes, particularly in August and early September, they will strike casually at things meant to be eaten, but without making any serious effort to run it down. Speeding up your fly – a technique that works sometimes when fish are taking short – will probably not work now; they just won't bother. You will probably lose quite a few fish, but they are feeding, and they obviously like the fly, so keep trying. Some are bound to stay. On other occasions, if nothing is happening, or if they are taking short, slowing down your fly may be the answer.

Letting your fly sink to the bottom and allowing it to rest there for a few moments can sometimes get you a hit when you begin the upward retrieve – usually with a black, or predominantly dark, pattern.

The direction of the wind, in relation to the direction you cast, will often determine whether or not you catch fish. Cast across the wind, and slightly into it. The line, pressed by the water, straightens, creating a natural, and enticing, movement of the nymph.

Casting directly into the wind will also have its moments, and its success. Casting with the wind is easier, but not necessarily effective. That doesn't mean to say it never is. There will be times when it is the only productive method; the food on which trout will at that time be feeding are free-moving creatures, unaffected by wind direction or current flow.

The key to consistent success is flexibility. As the situation changes, so too must you. To get stuck with a particular technique is to invite failure.

28

It is possible that you will be going off somewhere on holiday, perhaps with your parents. Fishing will not necessarily be the primary purpose, but you may have the opportunity to fly fish there. Most of the rest of Europe knows little about fly fishing. You can fly fish in Scandinavia, but the really good waters are very expensive, and the rest aren't nearly as good as ours. The French make you buy two licences, and give you decidedly mediocre fishing. The Spanish have succeeded in ruining their own fishing, though there are rumours that somewhere in the mountains one may encounter a trout. Yugoslavia has developed fly fishing in places, such as on the Gacka, which can be productive, if expensive, with the angler paying for what is caught. Most of us like to gamble on ourselves, but this method denies us the opportunity.

If you are off to some place where you think there might be a chance to catch some fish, take your equipment with you. If you can manage a second rod, consider a telescopic. It's a lot easier to carry around than your longer more conventional one. Mine is a Shakespeare, which folds down to less than seventeen inches, and extends to nine feet. It is meant for a No. 6 line, but I use it very well with a No. 9 sink-tip – this would probably come as something of a surprise to Shakespeare. It has a little plastic case, and fits nicely into a fishing bag.

With space a consideration I take just the one reel – with the slow-sink line. It's hard to anticipate in advance what conditions are going to be like; getting it wrong is more usual than getting it right. If in a quandary, I'll take the two lines. It is possible to buy extra spools, using them with a different line wound on each; you then change spools as the occasion arises. In theory this sounds pretty good, but in practice I'm not too happy. You've got a greasy spool to carry around with you, and changing one for the other is bound to be messy. It is possible to carry the extra spool in a plastic bag, which will make things somewhat less mucky, providing the bag does not tear. If you need two reels, take two.

For travelling, I have a tiny aluminium fly box, with clips, that fits nicely into a shirt pocket. I try to select a variety of flies – if I am going into the vast unknown, I can't do more than guess, and hope that I have guessed a little bit right. A ten-yard spool of leader should do. Pack a scissors and the sheepskin patch for hanging the flies. It's amazing how little you actually need.

If you are going elsewhere within Britain, and you know there are trout waters at your disposal, find out what you are able in advance. The trout fishing periodicals list the still waters. Check to see what waters are in the area you intend to visit. You can write to them directly, even obtaining your permits in advance.

It is possible that you are visiting friends or relatives who are fishermen, and who can be very helpful. They might be familiar with the waters as a result of their own experiences, or they might be able to get information for you. You will, in any event, want to get all the data possible. Every water fishes differently, and though you may come to know your own lakes very well, a new one will present different problems for you. Having read this far, you will be able to cope very well, even with a new body of water, but life will be easier, and success that much closer, if you can get some clues in advance. Pop in to the local tackle shop for information and advice, and to buy any flies they might recommend. It will often save you time and lessen the amount of frustration that might otherwise have to be endured.

29

Trout are not the only fish that will take a fly; many other species will, too. If you should ever be visiting the United States or Canada there are many thousands of lakes, with species of fish unknown in Britain, but are great sport and good eating – bluegills, crappies, sunfish, and bass are some of them.

But you don't have to limit your fly fishing to fresh water. You can fly fish in the sea, and in estuaries, where it is possible to take even salmon and sea trout. Fly fishing in the salt water has many advantages. There is no day permit to buy, and no bag limit. There are none of the rules and regulations that exist on a still water fishery, both public and private. Start and stop when you like. The fish that you can catch are almost all good to eat.

You can fly fish from the rocks, the jetties, from the shore. Your flies here will need to be bigger than those you normally use in the lakes. Silver body streamer flies are often the most effective. Clean your rod and line, and wipe down your reel after you have used it in salt water, which is very hard on equipment.

You must be very conscious of the tides; your life could depend upon it – literally. There are usually two incoming tides in a twenty-four hour period – and outgoing ones. Around these shores when the tide comes in, it comes in fast, and if you happen to be on some rocks jutting out into the sea, you can easily get yourself cut off. Swimming for it won't be that easy, either – with powerful waves pounding against jagged rocks. Don't take the sea lightly, and you won't have any problems.

The local tackle shop will have tide tables, which explain when the tides are due on each day. Tides are determined by the pull of the moon, so predicting in advance is not a problem. Fish also feed on the incoming tides, important to you as a fisherman. Now there is about an hour – slack tide – when there is no movement. This is a good fishing time. When the tide retreats, so too will the fish, though there are almost always fish about near the rocks that remain indifferent to the comings and goings of the tides.

Estuaries can also be productive places, but be careful here, too. They can be areas of extreme danger. Find out before you fish. The Welsh Tourist Board in one place sent me to a nearby estuary. Fortunately I checked further with the local tackle shop who told me about two of their customers – two of their *former* customers – local men who knew the water well; they went out in their boat one day, which probably overturned, and swept the men away in the tricky currents sometimes encountered in estuaries. They found the body of the one man, but the other hasn't been found yet.

30

Let's talk for a few minutes about our still water lakes, and say again how fortunate we are to have them. One that you may have heard quite a bit about is Avington, down in Hampshire. It has become famous throughout the country and in places abroad, known for the big rainbow trout that have come from there. This includes the current record, of $20\frac{1}{2}$ lbs. There is a bigger one, still, in there – over 22 lbs. I saw him the last time I fished at Avington. He surfaced for a moment, showing most of his massive back. On that same day two fish of about eighteen pounds were taken near where I was casting, and one of ten pounds a short distance up the lake.

Fly fishermen come from all over the country to cast their flies into these waters that have become a legend in our own time. They often leave with some very big fish – six and eight and ten pounds – the smallest ones are in

A fly fisherman at King's Langley, Hertfordshire. No need to watch the fly.

the two-pound range. Not that it's easy fishing. While it's very heavily stocked – you can see the fish – that doesn't mean they're going to take your fly merely because it's on offer. They are highly selective, and offer a challenge that can defeat seasoned fly fishermen.

It was all started by Sam Holland, who had retired to Hampshire – or had meant to retire. He dug a lake out of the ground and stocked it with trout. People came along who wanted to fish in it, too. He needed more trout; when the hatchery who supplied him failed to deliver, he began hatching his own trout. By selective breeding he has been able to produce the biggest rainbow trout ever seen in the British Isles. From the start he has worked with Roy Ward, highly knowledgeable, and deeply involved, who manages the fishery. Easy-going and likeable, it's Roy you'll meet if you go down to Avington. He'll advise you if you need help. If you should

Howard Holland, right, son of Avington Trout Fishery owner Sam Holland, advises a visitor to the water. Try a green nymph.

The cast.

I've had a hit. It's on!

It's a nice one.

go down there during school holidays, you may also meet Howard Holland, Sam and Barbara's eleven year old son, who might also have some good tips. He generally has peacock feathers for sale very reasonably, contributed by the peacocks who live at Avington.

Latimer Park Lakes in Buckinghamshire is a pretty place. You don't expect to come across a water that seems so remote but is actually so close to London. The fishing is generally pretty good, and the fish are sometimes fairly good size. The people who fish it regularly often do well, but it takes a bit of knowing. There are actually two waters here – the Upper Lake, where you can fish from a boat if you want to, and the Lower Lake, more like a river. So you get a choice, with each body fishing totally different from the other.

Further up in Buckinghamshire is Church Hill, consisting of two lakes that hold a good stock of fish, with two pounds being about the smallest, and going up from there. These waters will sometimes produce best in the morning – going quiet for a time in the afternoon, then picking up again later in the day. Deep in a lovely valley, it can get pretty windy here. Be prepared for the wind, to be able to cast into it, and to take home a limit.

Kings Langley is a recently-opened lake in Hertfordshire, created by Graham Gaywood, in a park-like setting, and managed by Richard Osborne-Kirby who will be pleased to offer assistance. It is well-stocked, with a season extending from March to November. Everything flourishes here – insect life, fry, and the trout that feed upon them, whose flesh is bright pink and tastes very good. Nymphs do well here, and so do silver-body flies that suggest fry.

The Thames Water Authority has done a good job in the creation of lakes, particularly for those living in London. Barn Elms, which can be reached by bus or underground, is surrounded by big office blocks and flats, but offers a setting that is a refuge for many kinds of birds, including Canada geese, ducks, and even hawks. It also fishes well. One lake is boat only. The other lake is reserved for bank fishing. It is well-stocked, but fishing isn't easy, and despite its bowl-like construction fishes like any natural water. Londoners are very fortunate indeed to have such facilities at their disposal.

On the other side of London, to the east, lies Walthamstow, a water that I have never fished, but which, I am told, is quite pretty and has produced some very good fish.

90

In the west there is Kempton Park, and the fairly new water, Farmoor 2, in Oxfordshire. There is also agitation to establish Hilfield Reservoir near Barnet as a trout fishery, and by the time you read this, it may well have happened. If it hasn't, it's going to be up to you to make it clear to the Thames Water Authority that you would like a trout fishery here.

Down in the New Forest Leo Jarmal runs the water he calls Leominstead.

It is a pretty place, and if you were to see it in the spring when the rhododendrons are in bloom, you would say it was a beautiful place. Leo keeps it well stocked and feels disappointed if his rods don't catch fish. They usually do. He had given up life in the city to get away from it all, and while he has succeeded in making his escape from the Big Smoke, he has become deeply involved in fishery management and the problems that face a fishery. He lectures on fishery management, and has made an outstanding contribution to the sum total of our knowledge.

The water is a dark peaty colour, which does not appear to have affected the fish's seeing ability. To avoid cutting down the trees that cover much of the bank side, Leo has built platforms out into the water. It works out very satisfactorily, however, making it possible to reach virtually every part of the water with your fly.

Stafford Moor, in North Devon, is also a very well-run fishery in a pretty setting. It holds good stocks of fish, some of them quite large. For me, it was a life saver the year of the drought, when the rivers I had considered fishing were well down, producing little by way of fish. I was pleased to return to it some years later to find that it fished better still.

The Midlands are rich in waters filled with fighting trout: Packington, where no bag limit is imposed. There are several lakes from which to choose, and you can fish from a boat or the bank. Eye Brook does not in theory have a limit, either, but they think that sixteen fish should be enough for anybody in the course of a day, and I can't argue with that. The fish are real scrappers here. Grafham Water is a well-established phenomenon, which has produced big brown trout from small stocked fish. It is 1600 acres, and takes some learning to be successful here. Its new

A well-satisfied fly fisherman at Avington.

big sister, Rutland Water, is 3000 acres. It has had its teething problems, and there was a lot of dissatisfaction early on. Apparently mistakes were made, and we hope that by now everything is straightened out.

31

If you have a camera, bring it with you to make a permanent record of those precious days. I don't know how much you know about photography, or how involved you are prepared to become. But the more you know, the better your pictures will be. A simple camera may not be difficult to operate, but the results may not be what you would like. Or there may not be any results at all. The camera can be likened to your eye. But, unlike your eye, you have to tell it what to do. With a simple camera there isn't much you can tell it, since there isn't much it can do. It has many limitations, and while it functions satisfactorily in ideal conditions, when things are less than ideal, you could have problems. Light conditions, particularly at the end of the day, are often not good. The fewer limitations you impose upon yourself, the greater the scope for taking your fishing pictures.

I use a Rollei 35, and have for many years. I can usually manage to get the pictures I want with it. I like it particularly because of its size. It closes down to where you can fit it into a shirt pocket. On the other hand, a single lens reflex is more versatile, though bigger. It allows you to see your picture as it will actually appear.

You will probably want photographs that provide you with colour prints. Or you may prefer slides, from which prints can now be made quite satisfactorily. Slides you see through a viewer or project on a screen.

Before you decide on a camera, do a lot of looking around, visiting camera shops and getting the opinions of people who are knowledgeable. Always remember, you are spending your money, so you should have the best possible value for it.

32

It's time you started to tie your own flies. Don't be frightened by it and don't be put off. It's not frightening and it's not difficult. You don't have to be particularly good with your hands, either. Your first efforts might not be your best, but the chances are very good that they will catch fish. The fish are a lot less fussy than the fishermen, and they are the best judge.

Once you get the feel of it and see what you can actually do, you may want to branch out on your own, and start tying your own creations. Do it! The chap who showed me how and said to keep tying the same pattern until I get it perfect before going on to the next one was no doubt correct, but I found it much more fun to do new patterns. The excitement of it all when they took fish was absolutely overwhelming. It may be for you, too.

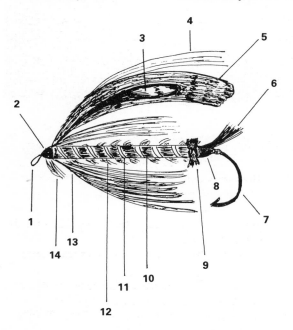

1 Eye of Hook
2 Head
3 Cheek
4 Topping
5 Wing
6 Tail
7 Bend of hook
8 Tag
9 Butt
10 Body
11 Ribbing
12 Body hackle
13 Hackle
14 Beard

Fly and Hook

Learn the names of the components of the fly, and the hook to which it is attached.

94

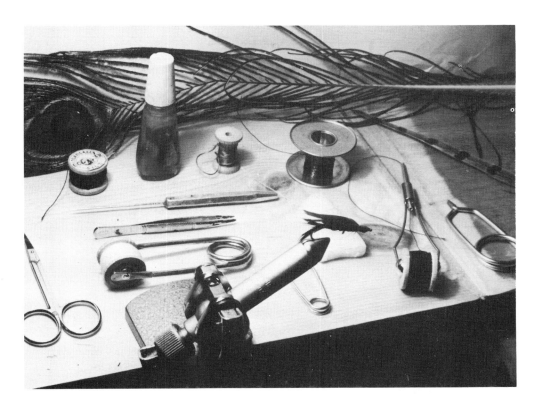

The Tools of the Trade

The vice: You want one that will hold all hook sizes, from the smallest to the biggest.
Sharp scissors; tweezers; bobbin; the needle-like device is a bodkin.

Hackle pliers; used for winding feathers, and holding them in place while you are attending to some other part of the fly.

Bee's wax: you can buy at the chemist.

Varnish: cheaper in large quantities, which you can then put in a nail-varnish bottle. If it becomes too thick for use, add a little turps substitute.

Buy your thread in full spools, the thinnest and toughest you can find, and wind onto smaller spools.

Tying flies creates something of a mess, bits and pieces of feathers that seem to have a life of their own. They go floating about, eventually coming to rest on the floor, attracting dust, and resisting all but the most serious efforts to sweep them up. Tape a plastic bag under your tying vice and sweep all bits of waste into it. Keep a brush handy. Dispose of all waste and cuttings immediately, and after you are finished, clean up.

Tying the Basic Fly

This is not a specific fly, but represents the basic tying. Follow these steps – it isn't difficult – and you will have the essence of fly tying. You will be able to follow instructions for specific flies, or make up your own.

Wax your thread. This is important. It will provide a solid grip onto the hook, and a secure tying that will hold firmly. For wet flies – flies that sink – you will generally want to use 'down eye' hooks, while 'up eyed' hooks are for dry flies – those that you wish to float.

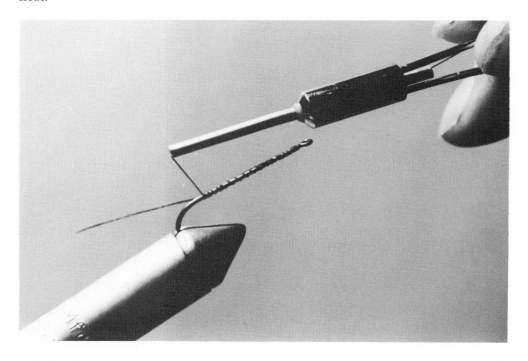

With the hook secure in the vice, run a strand of thread the length of the hook, from the bend (at the back) to the eye. Wind the thread over the strand from the eye back to the bend. Snip off the odd piece that remains. Always get rid of the bits that are not going to be a part of the fly as soon as you are able. You have now created the base for whatever tying you intend.

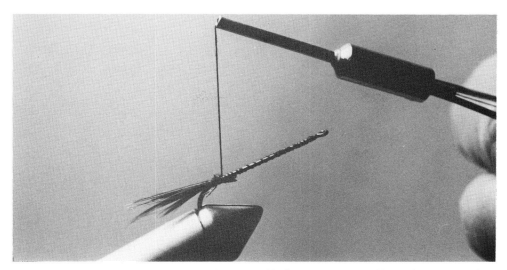

Attach the tail. In this case we are using the tail of a pheasant. Hold the feathers at the bend of the hook with your fingers, wind the thread around it several times, making it secure.

Now we are going to wind in the body. It, like the tail, and the components of the rest of this fly, will have come from that one pheasant tail. Wind the body feathers on securely, starting up the shank of the hook, and winding back toward the tail. Wind your thread forward to the eye.

Wrap the feathers around the shank of the hook, advancing ever forward to the eye. At this point, tie down the feathers at the eye, and trim off all the excess bits of feather.

Attach the wing. These are the bits of feather at the top. You tie it in as you did the tail, deciding how long and how thick you want it to be. Do the same with the beard, underneath. Make a number of turns with your thread, securing all the feathers tightly. Now for the knot at the eye that holds it all together. It's important to get it right and make it secure, since this is where it can all come apart. It is quite easy to do, follows naturally, requires no special skill, and holds forever.

With your index finger and thumb raise the tying thread about five cms. forming a loop. Bring the tying thread around the hook at the eye, raising it up as in the illustration.

Catch the thread, which has been brought up, with the index finger. Bring it through the loop, pulling it. This will form a new loop.

Pull it until the old loop forms a part of the head. Bring the thread around towards you. Catch it up again with your index finger, and repeat the process. Do this a third time. Take that third and final loop, slip it over the eye of the hook and tighten.

Cut the thread. Varnish the thread at the eye and allow to dry. This is your completed fly. Experiment, and create variations. If you want your fly to sink more readily, tie in copper wire, over the thread that you wrapped around the shank. Or you can use the wire stripped from pieces of electric cord. This wire can also be used as ribbing, tied around the body of the fly, which you tie in at the tail, and bring forward around the body.

That wasn't difficult, was it. Now you're on your way.

33

The best thing you can do for yourself as a fly fisherman is get your casting down right. It's more than practice – because if you don't do it right from the start, you will just be practising the wrong thing. The result will be that you are highly proficient at doing it wrong.

You will see fishermen struggling with the rods, as if they were trying to cast out giant weights into the sea, propelled by all the force they can bring to it, some of them turning their heads to and fro, apparently keeping their eyes on the fly. This method will insure that one gets tired quickly, becomes dizzy, and develops a crick in the neck. As mentioned before, it's all in the wrist. There is absolutely no need to turn one's head to watch the fly. If it has been tied on properly in the first place, the chances are it won't come loose from the leader and sail off somewhere.

Starting out: This is the grip, the thumb forward on the handle, the other hand holding the line.

Bring the rod up, keeping the thumb in the same position.

Do not bring the rod back over your shoulder, but keep it fairly straight, as in the picture.

Bend at the elbow, and keep the power in the wrist.

Bring your wrist forward, pushing on the rod to create power. This process is repeated in order to feed out line, and is known as false casting. Your line will curl behind you, then straighten out. Turn your head around and watch the process. It's a question of timing and coordination.

Bringing the rod forward at the moment the line has straightened out behind you, will create the momentum.

The line will shoot out, and land on the water, ending as you began. Now you are ready for the retrieve.

Having observed the process of the back cast, do not make it a practice to watch the line behind you. There is no need to do so, though you may have seen it done; it can only serve to make one dizzy and tired.

Proper fly casting is graceful, and because of its grace, very satisfying. Brute force or strength is out of place here.

Bear in mind that you want to transfer power from your rod handle to the rod tip, which you will do by your wrist movement. Think it. Concentrate on it.

34

Let's make our own rod. Here's how:

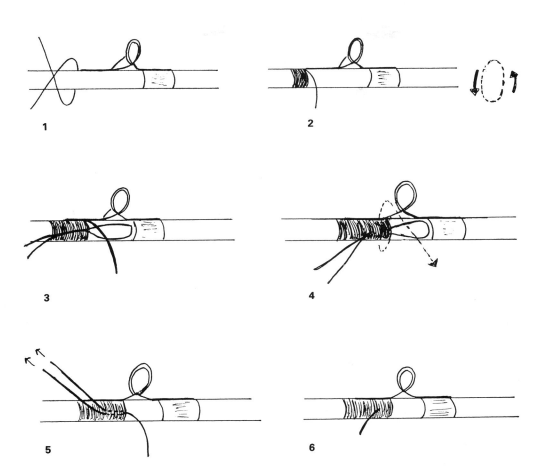

Making A Rod

There is no need to be hesitant about assembling your own rod. It is more daunting from the distance than it is when you get right into it.

You have selected your blanks, perhaps with the help of your dealer. You've got the rod rings – perferably the bridge type, as opposed to the snake – one for each foot of rod, plus the tip, and a single keeper ring; the reel seat, which you can buy, and the handle, partly-finished or all-finished.

You need some Gudebrod Rod Cement or Araldite, and a hundred yards of Gudebrod nylon "D" whipping thread. The thread is available in a variety of colours – and multi-colours – so choose the one that suits your rod best.

Regarding ferrules – I prefer the spigot type, rather than the metal. And make sure your reel seat has locking rings that thread closed as opposed to the rings that merely slide over the reel feet.

The part that some people find daunting is the wrapping of the rings onto the rod. This takes a little practice, simply because it is a completely new venture.

Check your blanks to see if one side is better than another, which is where you will want to attach your rings. File down the underside of your ring feet, so that when the whipping thread goes over them there will not be a giant bulge.

It's a good idea to have some practice runs, which will bring a large measure of confidence in doing the real thing, and helping to make the operation a fairly smooth one.

Tape down the upper foot, of the bottom ring, with sellotape. Now, with your practice thread, do the whipping as many times as might be required for you to feel comfortable at it. When that happens, we can go to work in earnest.

Okay? Start the winding about a quarter of an inch below the ring foot. Lay the thread down on the rod as if it were one leg on an X, holding it down securely with your left hand. Bring the thread under the rod with your right hand, and over, crossing the first thread to form the other leg of the X, as you see in Figure 1. Do this twice more, in order to bind down that starting thread firmly.

Roll the rod away from you, as in Figure 2, following the arrows, winding the thread on as evenly as you can. Cut off that tail. Hold the spool reasonably tight in your right hand, and roll the rod slowly with your left hand, pausing, when necessary, to make the newly-wound thread even.

Get on to the ring foot and go about half-way up it. Take a piece of thread about ten inches long, of a different colour, doubling it over, and loop-side to your right, as in Figure 3. Wind your whipping thread over it, and continue to wind to the edge of the ring.

Snip your tying thread, leaving about four inches. Bring it over the rod, from behind, and slip it through the loop. Figure 4.

Take a firm hold of the end of the looped thread, and pull sharply, so that it is no longer bound to the rod. Figure 5. This will firmly anchor the end of the tying thread, leaving you with only the tail exposed, Figure 6, which you then cut off.

Remove the sellotape and do the same thing with the other foot, and all the rest of the rings, until completed. The tip is stuck on with Gudebrod Rod Cement or Araldite.

Attach the keeper ring, just above where the handle is to be affixed, in the same way as the other rings.

Give your rod two coats of varnish, which you apply with your fingers. Apply three coats of varnish to the whipping.

Glue the reel seat to the handle, and the handle to the rod. When it has dried thoroughly, your rod is ready. The mystery of it all has disappeared. You are a rod builder. The rod you build yourself is indeed a very special rod.

35

If you have a bird – a pheasant, duck, or any other kind, for that matter – or a hare or rabbit, save the whole cape or skin, and use it as required for tying your flies. Here's how to do it.

Remove the legs, the wings and the head. With a sharp knife or thin-bladed cutting tool, cut upward from the vent, slowly and gently, prying the skin loose from the body. Be careful not to cut the flesh of the bird or animal.

The skin will peel off under firm pressure. If your skinning technique is at first a bit rough, don't worry too much about it; it will improve with practice.

It the head contains fur or feathers that you wish to retain as part of the skin, do not cut it off, but separate the skin from around it.

If the bird is a duck or goose or other water bird, there will be a goodly amount of fat attached to the skin. You will have to scrape it off. Pin the skin out on a board big enough to hold it in its entirety. You can use drawing pins or map pins for this. Stretch the skin as far as you are able, without tearing it.

Sprinkle generously with salt that is not free-flowing. In about a week your skin will be ready, and you have a large supply of feathers or fur for tying your flies.

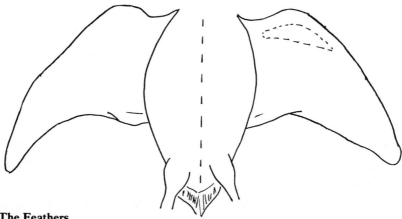

Keeping The Feathers

Cut along the dotted line as shown.
   Wings can be a bit tricky. It might be easier in some cases to cut off the feathers you want and dispose of the rest of the wing.

36

If you are away fishing for some time, and cannot keep your fish cold, the thing to do is salt them down, which will preserve them satisfactorily. Here is how you do it.

Get a plastic bucket, the bigger the better. Hopefully, you are going to be able to fill it. The salt you need is *non* free-flowing, which draws the moisture from the fish. This is important. Cover the bottom of the bucket with it.

Your fish have been cleaned and filleted. Lay the first of them, flesh-side down, on the bed of salt. Cover them up with salt, and add another layer, which you cover with more salt, repeating the process until your bucket is full or all of your catch processed. You can add fish to the bucket as they are caught, alternating layers of fish and salt.

Keep the bucket of fish someplace cool and dark. If you will be returning home within a fortnight, and you intend to freeze your catch, there is nothing more to do until then.

Upon returning home, clean your fish with cold running water, then cover with cold water and soak overnight. Rinse them again and dry. Pack them the way you find most convenient, and store them in the freezer, cooking in the usual manner.

If you are going to be away for an extended period, or if you don't have freezing facilities, then you will want to brine your fish. After seven to ten days of sitting in the bucket of salt, remove the fish and get rid of the liquid. Scrape off any salt formation or foreign matter from the fillets. Boil water, pour salt into it, and continue to add salt until no more will dissolve. Allow to cool. Put your fish back in the bucket and cover with the brine. Place butter muslin over the bucket, and keep it cool and dark.

It should remain in the brine for about two weeks. It is now ready. If stored in a cold place it will keep for about six months. Use it as required, soaking it first in the manner explained above.

37

If you love smoked salmon, you will love smoked trout even more. Doing your own isn't hard. The bigger the fish, the better. They should be two and a half pounds and up, though if you don't happen to have bigger ones, small ones will have to do. They won't be less good taste-wise, but the salting process, prior to smoking, reduces the weight of your fish to about half, which will mean that you've got an awful lot of bones, and not very much flesh.

However, as far as I am concerned, some is better than none. I have smoked smaller fish when I didn't have bigger ones.

It takes thinking about, and preparation in advance. First you need a smoker.

Remember, we are talking about *cold* smoking now – as opposed to hot smoking, which is merely another way of cooking your trout. A considerable amount of confusion has grown up around the two forms, with many people unable to distinguish one from the other. A little metal box with some sawdust inside, and a fire outside, does the hot smoking. All very nice, but your trout is merely cooked, with the smoke flavour added.

With cold smoking there is no flame, and your trout does not get cooked. You eat it raw.

Now, about that smoker – which you should be able to make yourself. The idea is to construct a box, about six feet high, which will stand on bricks, or legs, about eighteen inches long. At the bottom of the box you want a hole, so the smoke can enter. At the top you want a lot of little holes, for the smoke to leave. Up toward the top you want a bar, for hanging your fish while they are being smoked – or two bars if you are going to do a lot of fish. At the front you want a door so that you can put the fish in, and close up the smoker when it's being used.

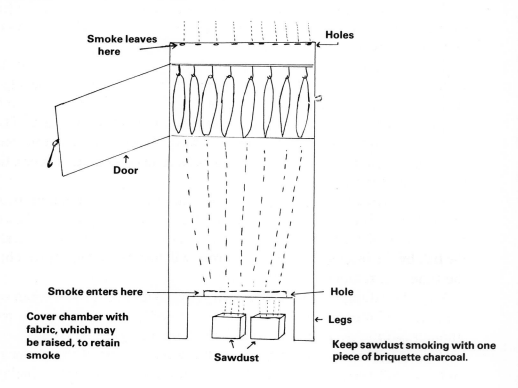

108

Sawdust or shavings are used for making the smoke. It should be from a hardwood tree – soft woods are resinous, and will make your fish bitter. The sawdust is meant to smoulder and create smoke – but never fire.

Get a piece of charcoal going, preferably a brickette, using, if necessary, a firelighter. Drop the charcoal on a bed of sawdust, blowing on it from time to time if necessary. You will ultimately need another piece of charcoal or two to complete the smoking. The sawdust will need replenishment periodically, with an additional handful dropped over the charcoal.

Keep your trout in the freezer until you have a sufficient number to smoke. Defrost completely. Fillet your trout, using those Snips mentioned earlier, or a kitchen scissors. Don't bother removing the bones at this time, since doing so will be very much easier after your fish is smoked.

To your salt – *not* free-flowing, which is meant to draw the liquid from the flesh – you can add crushed cloves, garlic, powder, crushed bay leaves, and brown sugar. Mix thoroughly.

Cover a plastic tub big enough to hold your fish with a layer of salt. Lay your fillets onto it, skin-side down. Cover with salt, and lay the next lot of fillets flesh-side down. Repeat the process with all the fish you intend to use. It is not necessary to do a large number of fish simultaneously. There is no downward limit; it depends how many fish you've got, the size of your smoker, and your facilities for storage. You can smoke just one fish, if that's all you've got.

If your fillets are two pounds or under, allow them to remain in the salt for six hours. If they are bigger than that, give them nine hours. The tub will begin to fill with liquid, which is the moisture drawn from the flesh of the fish by the salting process. Your trout will lose about half its wieght by the time you remove it from the salt.

After the salting is completed, wash your trout in cold water, then soak it for five minutes in cold water. It is not really necessary to dry trout (though salmon needs to be dried before smoking).

Hang it up in your smoker, through the boney part of its tail, or just under the gill case, which should be left on if the fish is meant for smoking.

Sid and his home-made smoker. It can handle twenty-four sides of trout at a time.

Check it from time to time. You may want to use two biscuit tins for providing smoke, insuring that there is an abundance of smoke, and that at least one is always in service.

The smoking process takes about six hours, but can be more or less, depending upon how much smoke you have got coming through. Timing isn't critical, but you can oversmoke, which will make your trout softer than it should be. This may not be so nice, but isn't actually a disaster. When it is ready, you will notice a moist covering on the flesh. Cut off a piece of trout and eat it. Does it taste right? Then it is.

110

The smoking completed, bring your fish in, and air out overnight in a well-ventilated kitchen. If you have smoked a goodly number, you will want to store them in the freezer. Wrap them in a double layer of cling film, which you can seal by touching the ends to a hot iron (covered in aluminium foil, in order to keep the cling film from sticking to the iron).

You have now provided the family with a taste treat that, in all probability, they will like so much, that they will make every effort to insure that you spend a lot of your time fishing.

38

Conclusion

Well, we've come to the end – the end that's just the beginning for you. You know what you need to know, and you are ready. The water is waiting for you. The dawn has broken, and it's a good day, a good season – and a good life. Enjoy every minute of it. I'm sure that you will.

We're bound to meet again, on the bankside perhaps. I'll be eager to hear how you have been making out. Good fishing. Good luck. I've enjoyed being with you.